Mahin Driskill

HOW TO ENTERTAIN BEAUTIFULLY

Mahin Driskill

HOW TO ENTERTAIN BEAUTIFULLY

Moods and foods to inspire and delight your guests

RED CAP
Publishing

How to Entertain Beautifully. Moods and foods to inspire and delight your guests
by Mahin Driskill

Red Cap Publishing
30 West Quay
Abingdon, Oxfordshire
OX14 5TL
U.K.
Tel.: +44 (0) 1235 533 939
info@redcappublishing.com

Find us on the web: www.redcappublishing.co.uk
Author's blog: www.mahindriskill.com

Photo of Mahin Driskill: www.dahlenphotography.com
Cover design & food photography: Kevin Wooding, www.15secondart.com

ISBN 978-0-956885-79-1

Printed and bound in the United Kingdom

"This is not an ordinary cook book.
Mahin has a special gift, and a couple of secret ingredients.
Her meals are prepared with unconditional love.
This book is offered from the same consciousness,
and that's why you'll notice the difference in your results
as you test her recipes and benefit from her experience."

Terry Tillman
Recovered Businessman, Scout,
International Leadership Trainer, Mentor & Speaker

ॐ

"Mahin never ceases to inspire
with her creativity and simple ideas.
Her recipes are both a treat to savour
and a feast for the eyes."

Noël Kingsley
MSTAT Alexander Technique

ॐ

"I have a wide taste in food and
eat almost anything, anywhere in the world,
but I've never tasted food like Mahin's.
There are so many delicious flavours
it feels like every single taste bud is being tantalized."

Gita Sootarsing
International Biodanza Facilitator

Contents

Introduction

"Good food, good wine and good company enrich our lives beyond measure" – Stephen Fry

What is home entertainment? Why would I entertain at home? These are the questions I once asked myself, long before creating this book. As time passed and I began entertaining at home, my initial reluctance gave way to a growing sense of wonder, and the answer to those questions came. Entertaining at home is an expression of love, it enhances my relationships and ultimately my life, and it can do the same for you.

My simple message is: make your guests feel special. To do that, you don't have to be perfect, just thoughtful.

Dear Entertainer

A very warm welcome to my book.

Entertaining can be enjoyable and fun - or even 'entertaining is enjoyable and fun' - particularly if you entertain at home. It is like music. It's what you do between the notes that count. Food and drink contribute to a party, but you are the one who makes it a truly great time for all.

This book touches on all forms of entertaining, from the setting you create to the food you provide. You are the one with creative control, the artist and the orchestrator.

Included is a brief introduction to the amazing world of colour to encourage you to experiment with the ambience of your home. Enticing food, colourful garnishes and delightful drinks will produce a beautiful table. Look to the astonishing marriage of colours in nature for new ideas that invite your guests to engage all their senses – the colours, the aromas, the textures and the tastes will help your guests relish the occasion.

The main part of this book contains versatile and international recipes which can inspire you to create your own delightful and wholesome signature dishes. Tips and suggestions based on my experience as a nutritionist and well-travelled caterer are included, as well as handy hints on menu plans, drink suggestions, garnishes and presentation. I want you to tap into your own creative flair and have fun, no matter how small your budget or how new you are to the world of home entertaining.

You can add that wow-factor to your party, whether entertaining family, friends, business acquaintances … or even your lover. You can make any occasion stylish whether cooking for a large crowd, a gathering of a few friends for supper or tea for two by adding your own special touches.

If you are a stranger to the kitchen and to the world of home entertaining as I once was – or you feel this is a big challenge with your existing lifestyle – try it out first weekly or monthly, when you can "practise", and then later you can handle that special occasion with ease and make entertaining a way of life. I'm sure that when you succeed once, you will want to do it again. As you entertain at home more, your gatherings will become memorable with unique personal touches and your self-confidence will grow.

I hope this book will bring wonderful changes to your life, and that it brings joy and pleasure to all those who share your get-togethers.

Planning & Preparation

"Success is the sum of details" - Harvey S. Firestone

A party lifts us out of our daily routine. It is a celebration, bringing gladness to the hearts of our guests and ourselves. Having a party should be fun and not hard work. Careful planning is the key.

Planning starts in your mind and not a few hours before your guests arrive. This will ensure your event is a huge success and prevent you serving up flat champagne, limp canapés, ill-thought-out conversation or even a disheartening atmosphere. A bit of forethought will help you to stay within budget, save you post-party regrets and wasted hours thinking about what you should have done.

Start with the end in mind.

Imagine your guests leaving your event. It's been a sensation. What do you hear them saying? What is your end goal, your definition of success? As you consider all the elements to achieve what you want, work your way towards your starting point. Be specific because this will become your route map to that successful end goal if you want to hear your guests say, "wonderful!"

It doesn't matter how large or small your gathering is, make organizing it fun. Take time, be realistic about your budget and pay attention to detail because ultimately that is what will make the occasion memorable.

Biggest tips for entertaining at home:

* Keep it simple. So many people try too hard, creating a nightmare for themselves.
* Create a simple yet imaginative menu with your shopping done ahead of time.
* The very best occasions have a wow factor. This alone will make the event memorable and your guests happy because of the surprise element.

When you decide to entertain, consider the following:

* Choose a theme and how you want to dress your home, your food and yourself
* Decide your wow-factor
* Work out a budget
* Organize your guest list and send out invitations
* Have a checklist
* Plan your menu

Themes

Choose a theme, which will focus and simplify matters. Planning an interesting theme will make your event less work and more fun and could even stir a lively conversation, especially amongst your unacquainted guests. Here are a few ideas.

The Seasons

Capture the essence of Spring with bright green and yellow, the colours of the daffodil on your table, and a serving of tender spring lamb and new vegetables. Golden pumpkins and a variety of squash are the fruits of Autumn. A tasty roasted butter nut squash and ginger soup (page 99) will add interest to a menu, and mini pumpkins and butternut squashes will make a gorgeous table decoration. See my suggestion on page 17.

Themed Nationality Nights

Make it an Italian night on a warm summer evening with spaghetti and opera music.
Or for example create an exotic evening with a Persian menu such as:

- Baba ghanoush, served with warm roasted sesame pitta wedges - pages 70, 75
- Persian style chicken kebab - page 87
- Carrot and cucumber salsa - page 162
- Fragrant rice with mint and pomegranate seeds - page 133
- A platter of dates stuffed with marzipan and drizzled with dark chocolate - page 171.
- Or Persian almond macaroons topped with a dollop of cream and a few juicy berries - page 181

Enhance the occasion with Melodic Middle Eastern music played in the background
or any culturally themed evening of your choice, such as:

Burn's Night

Bring cheer to a grey January day by celebrating Burn's night with haggis, neeps, tatties and a lovely dessert of Cranachan (page 170) with Scottish music playing in the background.

Travel

You might lay your table with several breads and different cheeses from around the world, garnished with their little national flags and platters of juicy, colourful fruits.

Vacation

If you've just been on an exotic holiday, share your happy experience with friends by creating that country's atmosphere for your occasion. It doesn't have to be over the top. A couple of tropical drinks, local-style bread, a main course, a dessert or fruit platter, accompanied by music played softly in the background and perhaps a short video of your adventure.

Global

Prepare a menu with dishes from the four corners of the world – for example,

- ❧ a light French chestnut soup (see page 100),
- ❧ a Persian Chicken with orange, cardamom and pan-roasted peppers accompanied with saffron rice (see pages 116, 132) and
- ❧ a light fruity Cranachan, native to Scotland (see page 170)

Complete the ambience with a selection of music from those countries.

Informal

Serve 4 - 5 very small courses rather than the more typical three-course meal, see the example below taken from the chapter on Easy and Elegant Dips, Canapés, Light Bites - page 68.

- ❧ Guacamole – page 69
- ❧ Oven-roasted red pepper, red onion and feta cheese - page 72
- ❧ Aduki beans hummus - page 72
- ❧ Roasted sesame pitta wedges - page 75
- ❧ Salmon, crème fraiche and horseradish with crostini - page 78
- ❧ Lightly spiced grilled chicken bites - page 88

Match your menu with appropriate music. For example, salsa or jazz, depending on your choice.

Wow-Factor

It all starts in the mind. Visualise the sort of party you would love to attend, be it simple or grand, depending on your time, finances and imagination!

It could be a theme, a centrepiece, an ambience, or simply you creating the circumstances to act as a catalyst to something magical and memorable. What the wow-factor will be is up to you and your imagination.

Budget

Experience has taught me that, decorations aside, when it comes to food and drink, it is best to have a budget per head. By having a budget and deciding on a menu, you will avoid the panic-stricken dash for poor-quality frozen and special offer foods.

Guest List / Invitations

When you know your theme and have considered what wonderful food and drinks you'd like to serve, send out any necessary invitations in good time. Whether you invite your guests with an informal telephone call, a text message, a click of your mouse on Facebook, or even an elegant calligraphy invitation sent in the post, it's a sign of care to give your guests an idea of what is planned and what time the food will be served. In the case of a large party, let them know if there will be a buffet, particularly if you have a chosen theme, and add an RSVP along with the invitation so that you will have a clear idea how many people to cater for.

Checklist

If you are not a list maker, become one! Write down everything that needs to be done. This will help you to keep abreast of everything at a glance and help you retain a sense of order and calm, knowing that everything will be taken care of. Keep your Checklist / to-do list somewhere very visible (front of your fridge?) and refer to them often and tick things off as you progress. I highly recommend also that you start keeping a notebook with the preferences and reactions of family and friends, which will make future entertaining easy. Keep it near your cookery books and refer to it before you entertain again to remind you.

One Week Before:

- Ensure you have enough glasses, jugs, dishes, napkins and cocktail sticks.
- Plan how you are going to chill drinks (fridge, ice buckets, etc).
- Prepare a music play list, if you want to have music at your event.
- Ensure you know how many guests are coming and ask them about any special dietary requirements in advance.
- Organise and confirm all food and drink required.
- Stock up on bin bags and tea towels for the clear-up afterwards.

One Day Before:

- Decorate your room beautifully.
- Prepare the running order with estimated timings.
- Set aside a place for your guests to leave coats, bags, etc.
- Make sure you know what you are going to wear!

One Hour Before:

- Turn the music on.
- Check the lighting level is perfect.
- Check the arrival drinks are ready; be sure to include a few non-alcoholic drinks for the drivers amongst your guests.

Timing it right

When serving food and drink, the timing matters as much as matching your carefully-chosen courses and wines. You want to start your party on the right note. Hungry guests, getting tipsy on empty stomachs and maybe even becoming a little cranky, will not enhance the occasion. But neither is it a good idea to rush things and serve the meal too quickly.

Get in the mood! Have a drink and relax. After all, it's your event. The good energy of a vibrant host is contagious because it sets the tone of the party. Knowing that all is as well as can be leaves you carefree to welcome your guests with a heart-warming smile.

Mini butternut squash, oranges filled with tealights

The Ambience of Your Home

"Your home is the outer manifestation of your inner soul" – Carl Jung

Beautiful surroundings act on the soul, and the way your home is prepared to welcome guests sets the tone for entertaining. An attractive setting creates lasting, pleasurable memories for your guests and makes you feel good, so the time and effort given to creating a warm, peaceful atmosphere will be repaid a thousand fold.

Creating ambience is not just for special occasions and special guests. It is for you and your family to enjoy at all times. Every day in which your home is beautiful will help raise your spirits (especially true when you live alone) and of course, a peaceful home calms the mind and relaxes the body.

Let's consider why and how we create ambience and the different elements that contribute to the overall look and feel of your surroundings.

Creating Ambience

Being comfortable and happy in your home stirs positive emotions, security and optimism, and beautifying your home does not have to be lavish and laborious however it definitely requires thought, attention and love. Well placed lights can bring a sense of tranquillity, colourful candles radiate a sense of warmth, soothing music calms the soul; and flowers enhance and perfume any room with a wonderful aroma.

Each space in your home is worthy of respect. You do not need to live in a mansion to create ambient surroundings. A loving, generous atmosphere can be created anywhere. This is much easier than it might seem. You just need to marry your personal tastes to a few basic guidelines. Rather than going to great lengths, keep things simple. You want your family and guests to feel at ease. Too lavish a setting can overwhelm and threaten the feelings of intimacy that you are seeking to create.

The tips and suggestions in this chapter will give you various ideas on how to stimulate good feelings in your guests from the moment they walk through your front door.

De-Cluttering

The first step to improving your surroundings is to let go of things you no longer use or care about. Maximizing the space in your home allows you see your possession at their best. Clutter breathes chaos. It is not easy to face the day with optimism in a cluttered home full of dusty knick-knacks and old memorabilia or stacked high with unwanted books, papers and files. An ever-growing pile of dirty dishes is a big obstacle to the desire to cook another meal. The best reward for keeping your home tidy is that you can easily find the things you want, when you want them. This will save you unnecessary time and frustration spent searching for missing items.

Keeping your home clean and tidy also means you can host spontaneous gatherings – say, after a film or after the match - and you won't have to spend the first five minutes frantically tidying and apologising for the state of your home.

Colours to Set the Tone

Without question, colour affects our mood. It feeds and nourishes our senses and plays a significant role in our well-being throughout all phases of life, whether we're wearing it, surrounded by it or even eating colourful food.

Medical science has proved that different colours have various effects on our nervous system. Like musical notes, colour affects us, depending on which colours we select, the intensity of those colours and how we arrange them. We know instinctively that dark, drab and dingy colours are depressing and that light, bright colours are uplifting, inspiring and bring out the best in us - physically, spiritually, mentally and emotionally.

Bearing in mind their impact, have fun and use colours to create the mood you want for your occasion. For example, bold colours have a dramatic effect and create a distinctive style, whilst complementary colours have a calming effect. A colour scheme that is based on warm colours, such as peach or gold, feel friendly.

Choosing a colour scheme begins with thinking about your favourite colours. What combinations will work best to enhance your home? Remember, no colour is absolute. Its perception is created by its context. For example, red appears richer in colour when it is surrounded by green.

Below are some ideas on how the colour of your décor can play a role in setting the mood at your party and in your home, and I would highly recommend checking out table arrangements at some of the better stores near you for inspiration about possible combinations.

White

White - strictly speaking - is not a colour but a neutral and reflects all light rays and is therefore cooling and restful. This is the colour of purity and fresh snow. As a neutral, it goes with everything. White can be chic, refined or rustic. For example, icy white with rich green brings a touch of ceremonial greeting for more formal occasions. However, it can also be too sterile or bland and uninspiring on its own as too much white can make people feel cold. Team it with bright accessories and artwork, or balance it with an ice-blue colour scheme and a warmer colour from the red or orange colour family to suit your tastes.

Blue

Blue is the colour of sea and sky. It has a pacifying effect on the nervous system that causes the body to produce calming chemicals. This tranquil, soothing colour is well suited to a relaxed gathering after a hectic day. Its cooling influence is welcome in a sunny room, but if your home is north facing and a bit chilly, blue will only increase that "cold feeling". Balance it with warmer colours such as orange and warm yellow.

Red

Red is the most emotionally intense colour. It is associated with love, passion, energy and fire. In nature, red fruits advertise their ripeness. In spices, cayenne pepper implies heat, which is why many restaurants opt for red decor because it is an appetite stimulant.

Nothing sets the tone for intimate occasions better than choosing this warm colour, as it stimulates emotion. However, too much red can cause one to feel irritable and uncomfortable, so use it discreetly and don't overwhelm the senses.

Yellow

Yellow suggests sunshine, warmth and happy summer days. It is a bright and uplifting colour and a good choice for a gathering of close friends.

Orange / Peach

Orange and peach both bring a feeling of warmth, fun, liveliness and laughter. In particular, the joyful relaxation of orange is wonderful for flower arrangements and table settings.

Green

Green symbolizes nature. It is calming and refreshing and is an ideal colour for a mixed gathering of very different people.

Colour wheel

I would strongly recommend that you buy a colour wheel from any good art shop. It will give you endless ideas on which colours coordinate and can suggest combinations you never considered before. For example, purple with the yellow that you see in pansies can be used for a lovely, natural flower arrangement.

As any artist knows, there are three primary colours - red, blue and yellow. They are considered primary, or true colours, because they are not made up of other colours and are used to make all the other colours of the rainbow. For example, red mixed with yellow makes orange; blue and yellow make green; and red and blue make purple. This is why orange, green and purple are termed secondary colours.

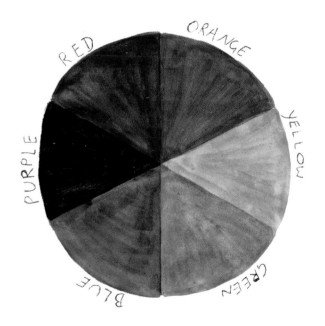

There are no good or bad colours and each colour has a complementary or opposite hue. For example, orange is complementary to blue, green is complementary to red and purple or violet is complementary to yellow.

To establish continuity in terms of colour and décor for your occasion, choose one main colour and select one complementary accent colour and one neutral (white, grey, black or beige). For example, if your tablecloth is blue, use white plates and choose bright orange or yellow flowers either on the table or in the room you use to entertain.

Setting a Beautiful Table

First of all, the shape of the table. The legendary King Arthur knew that seating his knights at a round table would help the flow of energy and ideas. An oval, round or octagonal table is less formal than a square or rectangular one. If your table is square, soften the edges by using a tablecloth. A round table is more likely to foster a lively conversation because it allows everyone to hear what is being said and therefore participate in the camaraderie.

TIPS:

- If your table is long and thin, avoid a wide and high centrepiece. Go for a low and colourful display.
- Place a runner cloth across the table instead of a centrepiece. This is especially practical with long, rectangular tables. Add candles along the length of the table for a warm, elegant appearance.
- Tables draped with a rich-coloured cloth can add interest.

The Colours on Your Table

A dining table laid with care makes any occasion less ordinary. Seeing a festive dining table stimulates our senses with delight as we anticipate the food to come.

The centrepiece for the table is a focal point and should incorporate beautiful colours but beware of colour overload. At the same time, avoid overloading your table - a small but elegant centrepiece can be overshadowed by elaborate dishes, candles or other items. Vary items at different heights and do make plenty of space for your eyes to rest.

SUGGESTIONS:

- To create a chic and more modern setting, pair your crockery with black and white accessories - black tablecloth with black or white vases and red flowers or napkins.
- For a stylish and simple setting, you could use green place mats and match them with fresh white tulips and their foliage in a rich green container.
- A rich source of inspiration is nature itself and its glorious seasonal colours. Draw on the colours of the season to make your setting more interesting:

Spring - marks nature's rebirth, so put together combinations of yellow, blue or just white and pink to welcome spring into your home:

- ❧ A pastel-coloured tablecloth; place mats with yellow napkins.
- ❧ Pink placemats with white napkins and pastel crockery.
- ❧ A pale green tablecloth accented with pink napkins.
- ❧ For flowers, bring in the fresh look of the new season to your table and home with the bright colours of tulips, hydrangea, daffodils and wonderful scented narcissus.

Summer – make your table pretty and welcoming with bright colours that reflect summer skies and flowers:

- ❧ White crockery teamed with different coloured glasses.
- ❧ A flowery tablecloth and a vase filled with country flowers such as purple coneflower, sweet peas or sunflowers.
- ❧ For a casual yet stylish setting, dress the table with a bright white linen tablecloth and make an attractive centrepiece with the palette of vivid flowers such as bright red anemones or red and yellow tulips.

Autumn - draw on bold and sensational autumn colours and festive harvest creations with colours such as burnt orange, rust-toned reds, browns and yellows accompanied with an accent of dark green, to bring the season's accent to your home:

- ❧ Make a centrepiece with twigs of red berries, acorns, orange pumpkins and leaves; drape your table with a chocolate brown, rust, gold or deep red tablecloth and complementary mixed coloured napkins.
- ❧ On your dining table add a brown, gold, sage green, or bronze table runner with a cornucopia of tiny gourds or squashes.
- ❧ Solid autumn colours for tableware and a darker shade of the same colour as place mats provides a soft accent and frames the plates and food.
- ❧ Add a warm touch to your autumn and winter table settings by drawing on colours. Tilt a simple straw basket on its side and fill it with citrus, nuts, colourful dried corn and pomegranates.

Winter - in deep mid-winter, bring into play cosy colours such as a deep red, burnt orange, a chocolate brown, a rich berry or a combination of these to create a warm welcoming ambience:

- ❧ Spread on the centre of your table plump twigs of red berries with tea light candles intermittently.
- ❧ Use dried fruit and vegetables as a centrepiece, wrap a piece of ivy around each napkin and around candlesticks, if you use them.
- ❧ Drape your table with a fuchsia cloth; contrast it with silver ornaments and bright white tableware.

- A table looks more charming if the setting is in a similar or complementary colour as the candles or flowers. For example, plain white plates sitting on bright orange placemats with blue candles, or earthy stoneware on rich olive green placemats, with yellow candles or daffodils.

TIPS:

- Take care when setting your dining table. Piled knives and forks in the centre of the table, alongside bland paper napkins or kitchen roll do not make a table attractive or inviting.
- A table cluttered with too many dishes can undermine all your efforts, so it's best to create a separate space for serving food, even if it means using a serving trolley.
- Remove empty serving platters as soon as possible so that your table always looks pleasing to the eye.

Place settings

If appropriate, small apples or oranges with a flag name tag make great place cards. These will brighten your table and make your guests feel welcome. You may double up your welcoming gesture by creating place cards that your guests can take home - for example, a tiny bouquet tied with a ribbon that has your guest's name written on it.

Attractive tableware

The colour, shape and size of your tableware can very much influence one's perception of a meal.

TIPS:

- The most elegant and versatile dinnerware is plain white porcelain trimmed with a thick band of gold, royal blue, jaguar green or rich claret. In general, any large oval or octagonal dinner plate in white or blue creates an elegant background to whatever you are serving, whether it is baked sea bass or a plain golden omelette.
- A colourful dish looks appetizing on a white platter, but a pale chicken salad in a light dressing looks much more tempting served in a rich colourful serving dish.
- Never serve the entire course on the same plate because it will make the plate look overcrowded and unappetizing.
- Serving platters are part of your table decoration, so it's worth paying a bit extra to select pretty oven-to-table cookware. You can bake, roast and serve in one container. It will keep your food warm and save on the clean-up time.

- Serve foods with a prominent colour in serving platters which have contrasting colours. For example, a carrot salad glows against a rich blue plate and a handful of strawberries look wonderful in a green or blue bowl.
- If you have only plain tableware, you can enhance the colours on your plate by garnishing and combining one coloured food with another. For example, fragrant turmeric and cinnamon rice will look very tempting next to chicken with orange, cardamom and sauce topped with pan-roasted peppers (see recipe on page 116). Always think contrast!
- Serve the starter on a medium plate and the main course on a large / extra-large plate so that each item of food has its own space to shine. Arrange the protein on top of the carbohydrate and sprinkle with a little garnish. Serve vegetables separately.

Lighting

"Give light and the darkness will disappear of itself"
- Desiderius Erasmus

Lighting affects the atmosphere in a room more than anything else, and the right type of light will give you the mood you want. Changing the feeling in the room can be as simple as placing softly-coloured light-bulbs in existing fixtures.

Choosing lights can be fun and there are many options. You can create cosiness or drama with carefully placed lighting.

SUGGESTIONS:

- Soft lighting can be created by placing a string of fairy lights around plants, along window ledges or strung across a bookshelf.
- Create elegant lighting by taping strands of coloured lights underneath a glass table and dress up your table with a very thin tablecloth to let the colours shine through.
- Fairy lights are available in a variety of different shapes and colours such as cubes, stars, lanterns and chilli-pepper shaped. They instantly make a room festive. The warm colours of Chinese lanterns lift the mood and generate a sense of the brightness of summer, no matter how gloomy it is outside.
- A disco-style mirror ball suspended from the ceiling makes an interesting play of light for a fun, informal gathering or cocktail party.

Remember that you want people to see the room and each other! It's difficult to converse with someone you can't see.

Then there is one of the oldest, most magical forms of lighting that exists and is a particular favourite of mine …

Tea light candles tucked in throughout cranberries

The Charm of Candles

"It is better to light a candle than curse the darkness"
– Chinese proverb

The love of candles is shared by many cultures around the world. Candles are versatile and lend elegance, warmth and intimacy to gatherings of any size. Candles create a sense of eternity and peace when it is cold and dark outside and candlelight casts a flattering glow around the garden as dusk falls.

At the table, candles can bring different feelings to the setting. For example, red and green candles give a classic, Christmassy touch; whereas tall gold or silver candles convey a modern look, and enticing, cinnamon-coloured candles enhance a relaxed and intimate setting.

TIPS:

- Mini pumpkins, butternut squashes, oranges and apples can be hollowed out to hold tea lights or short candles.
- Cut the top of the orange the size of a tea light. With a sharp knife, gently empty the orange and save the bits of fruit with the juice. Fill the top third of the orange with some foil to let the candle sit on top.

SUGGESTIONS:

- When hosting an informal get-together, use candles to spread focal points of light above and across the table. Fill small, inexpensive red, green, yellow and blue glass candle-holders with tea lights and place them around the floor at the edge of the room. Their glow radiates a sense of being immersed in a magical rainbow. (Please see Tip).
- Mix floating yellow, blue, pink and purple tea lights in a spacious, clear glass bowl half filled with water.
- Create a pretty candle centrepiece by filling a shallow glass bowl with cranberries and tuck in tea light candles throughout.
- Candles arranged in groups give a stronger impact.
- Mirrored surfaces reflect light - place candles on a mirrored tray.
- For a simple and impressive display, place candles on a piece of foil in the centre of a plate. Decorate the base with any greenery you have to hand - a swirl of ivy, bunches of bay leaves or handful of winter berries still on the twig.
- Candlesticks of different heights look effective when arranged together. Vary their heights by elevating them on inverted small bowls. Disguise the base with silver foil or greenery.
- Silver candlesticks, or candelabra, with large red or purple candles have a regal touch.
- Other ideal candleholders are wood, ceramic, terracotta and glass.
- Buying a pair of crystal holders may seem extravagant, but they look beautiful and will last a lifetime. When you light your candles, prisms of light will glitter onto the ceiling and every corner of the room will be enhanced by a subtle rainbow.

- When dining al fresco in the evening, aromatic candles light the scene and discourage biting insects with their smoke.
- A much forgotten and useful trick is to store your candles in the freezer before use. Chilled wax burns longer without dripping and your ambience will persist long into the night.

TIP:

- Make sure candles are placed in a safe spot away from draughts and not close to curtains or electrical wires.

The Gift of Scent

"Smell is a potent wizard that transports you across
thousands of miles and all the years you have lived"
– Helen Keller

Scent taps into the deepest recesses of our minds, evoking memories and deep-rooted emotions. We associate certain scents with feelings of being at home, with being in love or with feeling comfortable. Different scents provoke different feelings.

TIPS:

- In autumn, make your own attractive potpourri. Fill tiny pumpkins with cranberries, cloves and cinnamon sticks.
- Freshen a stale potpourri with a few drops of orange blossom or by adding cinnamon sticks and orange peel to the petals.
- Cut a few clementines in half and arrange them in a circle on a plate, surrounding robust coloured candles. The heat from this ornamentation will then infuse the air with the delicious aroma of fruit.
- Lightly spray grapefruit or rosemary on the curtains, cushions and upholstery, which will disguise the smell of food after cooking. You could also place a good quality potpourri in the corner of the room.
- Though a delicate scent indulges the senses, rich fragrances can be overwhelming, so it is important to be careful where you place perfumed flowers and scented candles. An ideal spot for strong scented flowers could be on the floor or close to the window where their aroma will mingle with that of the fresh air entering the room.
- Always consider your guests. Some people are highly sensitive to flower-based smells.
- The smell in the air plays a large part in any ambience and no amount of scent has the power to disguise heavy, stale air redolent of many past suppers. Every day, open your windows for a while, even in the middle of winter, to ensure that your house stays fresh and odour-free.

SUGGESTIONS:

- Many people associate the scents of cinnamon and vanilla with love, perhaps because our mothers used these delicious ingredients when they baked for us as children. Peppermint is among the strongest aromas for memory association.
- Citrus and rosemary add energy to surroundings, whilst floral scents create a feminine ambience. Exotic scents like sandalwood, jasmine and orange blossom create a sense of luxury.
- Hyacinths can fill a room with their exhilarating, distinctive fragrance. Their beautiful blossoms make a pleasing still life in the midst of winter, hinting at the coming glories of spring and summer even when there may still be snow on the ground.

Various vases filled with flowers

The Magic of Flowers

"A flowerless room is a soulless room, to my way of thinking,
but even one solitary, little vase with a living flower may redeem it"
- Vita Sackville-West

Flowers enrich our homes and exude a colourful and aromatic welcome. And with a little imagination, you can create an original table centrepiece such as a rose in full bloom surrounded by sprigs of fragrant rosemary; a bunch of purple lavender encircled with a cluster of aromatic mints, or a few bay leaves wrapped around winter red berries.

For your party, try keeping flower displays informal if that is in the spirit of the event.

Flower arrangements are not restricted only to centrepieces. Scatter the table top with tiny flowers or space them between glasses and ornaments.

A small bunch of flowers tastefully arranged and carefully positioned brings more beauty to your home than a bulky arrangement plonked in the middle of the table which may block the view of those sitting opposite each other.

Low wide vases are best for a table arrangement

You do not need expensive flower vases to display your flowers or to be an expert arranger.

A basic container can be transformed into a pretty flower vase, and any simple bunch of flowers can be displayed with flair.

TIP:

- Add a dash of lemonade or baby bottle sterilizing tablets to your vases to keep the water clear and make flowers last longer.

SUGGESTIONS:

- Fill a pitcher or a tea pot with daffodils or daisies to bring a touch of a fresh country look to the table.
- Place single flowers in small vases, or bell-shaped wine glasses and group them together for effect.
- Bring a sunburst of colours to your room with a rich blue or green vase full of bright, bold flowers.
- Use empty cans or glass jars as flower containers. Wrap them in pretty crepe paper tied with fine ribbons. Fill the containers with a bunch of sweet peas, daisies or poppies. Place marbles, or dried beans in the bottom of the container to hold your flowers. If you do not have crepe paper at hand, fill up the glass jar with a handful of colourful mixed beans - dried kidney beans, chick peas, lentils. This also helps to keep flowers upright.
- Pumpkins and butternut squash make attractive natural vases. Scoop out the centre and place damp florist foam or a cluster of pan scourers in the hollow with some water. Then fill these golden vegetables with a small bunch of pretty flowers and remember to slice off a thin section from the bottom of the squash to form a stable base.

Mini pumpkins filled with autumn leaves

The Ambience of Sound

"Music washes away from the soul the dust of everyday life" - Berthold Auerbach

Your choice of music will create or stifle the party mood. Soothing sounds create feelings of security and companionship. Natural sounds like the breaking ocean or a crackling fire in the hearth can induce a nostalgic glow.

Choosing music to entertain you is one thing. Selecting the right soundtrack for a party or dinner with guests is quite another.

TIPS AND SUGGESTIONS:

- Choose CDs before your guests arrive and bear in mind their likes and dislikes.
- Prepare a selection of music to play as your party evolves.
- Select music that expresses something about your personality and tastes, but also works well for the event that you are hosting. Instrumental music provides a beautiful sonic experience. For something smooth, consider easy-listening or blue grass country. The bubbling sound of jazz adds a lively backdrop to your party.
- Seasonal favourites can be fun for Christmas or other important holidays but don't go overboard. Appropriate as it may seem to play 'I'm Dreaming of a White Christmas' in December, playing it more than twice is unimaginative.
- Playing the top pop hits from your teenage years is probably a good idea if you are hosting a party with your age-group present.
- Remember that as much fun as it is to go down memory lane, self-indulgence risks irritating guests who don't share your tastes in music.
- When serving food with a distinctly ethnic theme, find music to complement the occasion.

The most important thing to remember is that we are affected by our surroundings. Your little touches show that you care about the occasion and your guests, and these will create a lasting impression of you and your home.

Delicious Drinks for all Seasons

"When a drink sings, the drinker smiles!"

Whatever the occasion and whoever the guest, a delicious drink that is beautifully presented says welcome like nothing else.

Serving something a little different with thoughtful garnishes adds a sparkle to your gathering - whether it is home-made lemonade on a hot summer day or a mulled wine with cranberry for finger-numbingly cold winter evenings.

There are a variety of recipes in this section, from punchy, colourful cocktails to refreshing, non-alcoholic thirst quenchers. You can make these for any number of guests, on any budget.

Attractive Drink Garnishes

Garnishes are the starting point to making your drinks look more enticing.

Armed with fresh ingredients - such as cherries, juicy berries, ruby red pomegranate seeds, delicate segments of lemon, lime, orange, olives, borage flowers and fresh mint leaves - and the desire to create, let's go!

TIPS:

- Remember to buy cocktail sticks.
- Bring sparkle to a chilled drink. Freeze: red and blue berries, mint leaves and curls of lemon and orange zest in ice cubes to float on top of drinks.
- Cut a couple of strawberries crosswise with their green stems on and lay in a slender glass. Fill with sparkling wine.
- Add puréed raspberries to sparkling wine to create a pink fizz.
- Decorate glasses with a couple of whole berries on skewers.
- If inclined, personalize your guest's glasses. The bonus is that guests won't lose their drinks and you won't be left with a pile of half-full glasses.
- Make pretty tags with your guests' names on them to go around the stem of glasses. The tags can be made from a colourful paper with a hole through it. Slide a piece of ribbon through the hole and tie it around the stem.
- Use whimsical wine charms. After your special event, you can continue to enjoy your charms on the handle of a coffee or tea cup and even beer mugs. Search for them on the Internet. There are amazing varieties out there.
- Cut your guests' initials into a citrus peel using alphabet cutters. Put cut peel into each glass. The alphabet cutters are available in most party shops and can also be used for shaping icing or marzipan to put on birthday cakes.
- Stick funny stickers on glasses, something to go with the theme of the party!

A Glass Act

What you serve is important, and so is what you serve it in.

Presenting drinks in the right glass can make even a simple cordial look more inviting.

Glass is best. Disposable cups have their place and can be useful if you are planning a casual party but do think about it. Paper cups do not catch the eye! They make every drink, from champagne to beer, look exactly the same. The rough touch of plastic on one's lips is much less sensual than lifting a cool champagne flute. And even the greatest wine loses its soul in a plastic beaker, while a modest wine may well impress when served in a pretty glass.

If you must use plastic cups, then select transparent ones rather than white plastic. At least clear cups will allow the drinks to look different and you can still make them look attractive.

The right glass makes all the difference.

When it comes to drinking wine and champagne, the shape of the glass is just as important as getting the temperature right. Buying glasses designed for their purpose is worth it, even if it means spending a little extra, if that is within your budget. It will help guests to taste drinks at their best and to enjoy the flavour and aroma and appreciate colour and texture.

Taste buds, which are located on the tongue, are stimulated by salty and sweet flavours. When we drink, the liquid activates different taste buds, depending on where it is deposited in the mouth. Narrow champagne flutes bring the wine to the front of the mouth, where sweet and sour flavours tingle, while broad-bellied glasses introduce red wine to the sides and back of the mouth, where the receptors for bitter and astringent flavours are located.

TIPS:

- The best wine glasses taper in slightly towards the top, which helps to hold the aroma of the wine in concentration so that you can smell it better.
- Tall, slim flutes display and prolong the bubbles in champagne and sparkling wine.
- Larger glasses allow air into the wine, causing the bouquet to be experienced at its fullest. The ideal wine glass is a generous tulip-shape with a slender stem. Most people use larger glasses for red wine and smaller glasses for sweet wine.
- Large wine glasses are for more than just wine. They can be impressive containers in which to serve light starters: prawn cocktail, chilled soup and colourful desserts like fruit salad, ice-cream, trifle or mouth-watering fruit jellies.
- When those pretty wine glasses are not being used to sip from, fill them with fresh flowers to make for pretty centrepieces on your table.

Caring for your glasses

Glasses are delicate vessels and benefit from a touch of tender, loving care.

When it comes to enjoying sparkling wines, the cleanliness and bone dryness of the glass are almost as important as the chill. The residue of detergent, the slightest trace of water or tiny bits of fluff from tea towels will kill the bubbles immediately.

TIPS:

- Wine glasses should be washed with detergent and then rinsed in hot clean water. Wipe and polish them while still hot with a cotton dish-towel reserved only for glassware.
- Store wine glasses properly, never upside-down. This is to prevent stale air from getting trapped inside. The stale and musty smell that accumulates as a result of incorrect storage can spoil the enjoyment of wine and is difficult to get rid of.

Grape Expectations

Enjoyment of wine includes the aroma of the wine and its taste.

TIPS:

- Many wines, and especially red wines, are best tasted after they have been allowed to "breathe" for an hour or so at room temperature. To increase the exposure of wine to the air, pouring one glass will let air into the bottle.
- Fill a wine glass a third or preferably half way full so that there is plenty of room in the glass for the wine's aroma to be enjoyed. This will leave enough room in the glass for the discerning drinker to appreciate the bouquet of the wine.
- In summertime, instead of putting ice cubes in a glass of white wine, try plastic ice cubes in a jug, which will keep the wine cold without diluting it.

Choosing your wine

Choosing the right wine will bring out the ingredients in your meal and enhance your dining pleasure. Acidity in food needs to be matched to acidity in the wine; otherwise the wine will taste dull and flat. White wines generally have higher acid levels than red wines, which have more tannin.

TIPS:

- As a starting point, try to match a delicately flavoured dish with a delicately flavoured wine. White wines are usually lighter-bodied than red wines and are typically served with lighter flavours such as fish and white meat, while red wines work best with meats, cheeses and more robust flavours.
- As well as considering the primary ingredient of a dish when selecting wine, think of what else is on the plate. For example, if a delicately flavoured ingredient is covered with a heavy sauce or cooked with a strong spice, you will need to find a wine that complements the taste of the sauce or the spicy flavours.

Matching wine to food

Red meat: Most red meats are best with a red wine, their tannins being softened by the meat. Red Bordeaux is a classic match for a well-aged steak, but do not overlook the less costly Spanish Tempranillo. Very simply, the richer the dish, the more substantial the wine. For the darkest beef or game, choose a red wine high in tannins.

White meat: Chicken and turkey have fairly delicate flavours. Choosing wine depends on the way the meat is cooked. Lightly grilled or in salads, white wines tend to be the best bet. Also lighter reds can work well with roast chicken, or if serving a strongly flavoured sauce.

Fish: The more delicate the flavour of the fish, the lighter the wine needs to be. With grilled white fish, try dry, zesty wines such as Pinot Grigio, Point Blanc or Muscadet. The delicate flavour of shellfish such as lobster, crab and prawns is complemented by very light wine. However the wine should be more robust with stronger flavours of fish such as tuna or swordfish and its accompaniment, such as a creamy sauce, the more robust the wine should be.

Pasta:

Choose light whites for seafood pasta and fruity reds for meaty pasta. For pizza and pasta with tomato sauce, try a hearty red.

Mediterranean, Middle Eastern and vegetarian dishes:

Rosé often goes well with these dishes.

Deep-fried fish, chicken and veal:

These taste best with an unoaked Chardonnay or Sauvignon Blanc.

With light stir-fries of fish, chicken or vegetables:

Serve dry Riesling.

Grilled food:

Grilled food may demand quite forceful wine because of its pronounced browning flavours. Choose a fruity red wine like Syrah or Shiraz for red meat, or a strong white wine for poultry and pork, like an oaked Chardonnay or a Semillon.

Simple roast meat:

Roast meat is ideally complemented by fine red Claret.

Where herbs are used:

Choose reds with a spicier character like a Rioja or a country wine from Puglia.

Champagne is one of the more versatile wines to serve with food and I would suggest serving with lighter foods so that it can be savoured fully.

Three major DON'TS when combining food with wine:

Combining wine with food is a matter of taste more than rules. There are, however, some don'ts and they tend to embrace most peoples' tastes. Here are a few:

- Avoid matching dry Champagne with desserts - food and wine combinations are very much about finding the right balance between both. Since dry Champagne is all about acidity and lightness, it doesn't work at all with puddings and sweets that are all about richness and sweetness. Dry Champagne with pudding feels so bitter and acidic. Go for demi-sec (medium sweet) Champagne, which will balance the wine in favour of the dish. Alternatively, use a medium sweet sparkler Italian off-dry Prosecco or Asti.
- Avoid using red wines, tannic red wines (Cabernet Sauvignon, Syrah, Malbec, Mourvedre, Tannat, Sangiovese, Aglianico) with vinaigrettes, lemon juice and sauces with high acidity.
- Red wines contain tannins. Some contain more than others and the tannic concentration really depends on grape varieties, climate / soils and winemaking. The effect of a wine with high tannins, if drunk with no food, will produce a feeling of roughness and dryness in the mouth. Also, acidity reinforces tannins on the palate, making the whole combination even more astringent. Generally fat (butter, cream, fat in meats, etc.) tends to soften tannins in red wines. If you use a structured red wine (with high tannins), use similarly structured food such as tight meat (beef, lamb) with sauces that will match the structure of the wine and soften the tannins.
- Avoid strongly-flavoured food with soft-flavoured wines - the flavours of such food would completely destroy the flavours of your wine. The same applies to garlic, which tends to "mute" most wines and certain spices! These ingredients / foods are difficult to match and require specific wines which will need to be very aromatic and hold the pairings such as the Riesling, or Gewurztraminer grape varieties in the case of spices.

Wine with sweet dishes

Sweet foods, other than desserts, should be matched with sweet wines. A dry wine served with sweet foods will taste bitter in comparison. Sweetness in a savoury dish is less obvious. You won't want a sweet wine just because there is sweetness from vegetables like sweet potatoes, carrots and onions, or from a sauce or relish. But any of these are likely to make red wine with strong tannins taste dry and harsh, and a light, dry white wine taste thin and sharp. The answer is the sort of ripe, full flavours that come from sunny climates, like a fruity red Primitivo from southern Italy or a soft Sauvignon Blanc from New Zealand. Think un-oaked French Chardonnay for salads, and aromatic Riesling from Alsace to counter creamy main courses.

Dessert wines

When it comes to puddings, there is just one rule - pick a wine that is as sweet as or slightly sweeter than your pudding. Chocolate is notoriously tricky. It copes best with sweet, fortified wines such as port, Muscat or Australian liqueur.

Wine with cheeses

See Cheese and Wine Parties, page 52.

Wines for the budget-conscious

Selecting a drinkable wine at a modest price is possible if you pay attention to supermarket bargains.

> TIPS:
>
> - Choose a wine that was produced close to an expensive region, but not in that region. For example, a white Burgundy from Auxerre will be as good as Chablis at a fraction of the price.
> - Select wines from small vineyards rather than a huge producer.
> - If buying French wine, choose one from an appellation as close to the wine producer as possible instead of a general 'appellation Bordeaux'.

Serving wine at the right temperature

Wine should ease the soul by encouraging another sip. Serving wine at the right temperature makes a big difference to the pleasure of the drink.

Other guidelines

Gas in wine: The higher the temperature, the greater the release of gas in the wine. If you drink a sparkling wine at room temperature you will feel a very unpleasant sparkle. This is why sparkling wines should always be served cold.

Tannins in wine:

Tannins will feel harsher at lower temperatures. This is why tannic red wines taste horrible when chilled. It should be served at room temperature. Lighter wines with lighter tannins should always be chilled.

Alcohol and sugar:

Alcohol and sugar feel heavier at higher temperature. This is why it is better to drink sweet wines at a cooler temperature.

> TIPS:
>
> - To chill your wine and champagne quickly and easily, put the bottles in a bucket of ice and water.
> - Always remember that even those who enjoy a drink with their meal will appreciate water and soft drinks being available, so keep some jugs filled with ice-cool fresh water.

Champagne - Sparkling Wine

Sparkle is an essential ingredient at a drinks party because it is the thing that puts everyone in a celebratory mood. Champagne, with its magic name, may be considered as an eternally festive and a timeless fun drink. But there are other sparkling candidates that are kinder to the pocket and particularly pleasing to some people who find champagne too dry or acidic. Cava from Spain and Prosecco from Italy are fruitier, softer and almost invariably sweeter. Whichever you choose, it has to be served chilled.

Champagne or Sparkling Wine with Crème de Cassis

This is a tasty, simple cocktail. Add a shot of crème de cassis to champagne or sparkling wine such as Prosecco or Cava.

TIP:

- Remember, because most sparkling wines are sweeter and less acidic than champagne, they can easily become over-sweet if you add too much crème de cassis. Much depends on the brand of sparkling wine, but you are unlikely to need more than one part liquor to seven of sparkling wine. And one to ten may well be enough.

Bellinis

Adding puréed peaches, or crushed raspberries to chilled champagne or sparkling wine makes a refreshing cocktail. Any of these fruit purées keeps well in the fridge for up to 3 days.

Peach Bellinis

Serves 5 - 6

    3 - 4 ripe peaches, peeled, stones removed, then puréed

    1 bottle of chilled champagne, Prosecco or Cava

Fill ¼ of champagne flute with the fruit purée.

Top up with chilled champagne or sparkling wine.

Raspberry Bellinis

Serves 5 - 6

    200 g (7 oz) fresh or frozen and defrosted raspberries
    1 bottle of chilled champagne, Prosecco or Cava

To garnish:

    A handful of fresh mint leaves

1. Crush the raspberries with a fork. Cover and refrigerate.
2. When ready to serve, place 1 tablespoon of the raspberries into a Champagne flute, then top up with chilled champagne or sparkling wine. Stirring gently to combine and garnish.

Sparkling Pomegranate Punch

This refreshing punch is made with tart sweet pomegranate juice and finished with sparkling wine.

Serves 12 - 13

    1 litre (1¾ pint) pomegranate juice
    500 ml (18 fl oz) fresh orange juice
    500 ml (18 fl oz) chilled lemonade

    1 bottle of sparkling wine such as Prosecco or Cava
    Ice cubes

To garnish:

    Lime and orange slices and a few pomegranate seeds

12 - 13 highball glasses

1. In a punch bowl, combine the pomegranate juice with orange juice and lemonade.
2. Just before serving pour in the sparkling wine.
3. Serve chilled over ice. Float lime and orange slices on top and sprinkle with pomegranate seeds

Mulled Wine

> **Tip:**
>
> - Never pour very hot wine into a glass. Place a spoon in the glass first and then pour the wine on to the back of the spoon. This reduces the shock which the glass would otherwise have to withstand.
> - For finger-numbingly cold winter evenings, a glass of mulled wine with its inviting aroma of warm winter spices and its delicious full-bodied flavour is just the thing! It is easy to prepare. The advantage for the host is that there is only one type of drink to serve and it is easy to prepare. There is no need to offer red or white wines. All you have to remember is not to overheat it and resist the temptation to over-spice. Here are two suggestions for making this winter drink.

Mellow Mulled Wine

Serves 6

1 bottle of full bodied red wine, 750 ml

300 ml (1/2 pint) water

175 g (6 oz) caster sugar

1 large cinnamon stick cut in half

Rind of 1 lemon thinly pared

To garnish:

One lemon thinly sliced into 6 - 7 slivers and pips removed.

6 small heatproof glasses

1. Make the mulled wine by simply placing all the ingredients in a large saucepan. Bring slowly to a simmer, stirring to dissolve the sugar. Cover the pan with a lid and allow the mixture to infuse over a low heat for 10 about minutes.
2. Turn the heat off and remove the cinnamon (see Tip 2 above). Taste the mulled wine and if it is a bit too sweet to your liking, add a dash of lime or lemon juice.
3. Place one slice of lemon in each glass. Strain the warm wine into the glasses.

Mulled Wine with Cranberry

Serves 10 - 12

1 bottle of full bodied red wine, 750 ml

1 litre (1 ¾ pint) cranberry juice

110 ml (4 fl oz) brandy, vodka or rum

1 orange cut into 4 - 5 segments

6 - 7 cloves

1 large cinnamon stick cut in half

To garnish:

A few cranberries and wafer thin orange slices

10 - 12 small heatproof glasses

1. Place all the ingredients in a large saucepan. Bring slowly to a simmer, stirring to dissolve the sugar. Cover the pan with a lid and allow the mixture to infuse over a low heat for about 10 minutes. Turn the heat off, and remove the cinnamon. See Tip 2 above.
2. Strain the warm wine into the glasses and garnish.

Sangria - The Juicy Punch

This refreshing summer red wine punch is delicious, looks beautiful and is easy on the budget. Above all, it takes little time to prepare.

Serves 12 - 14

Juice of 1 orange

1 small glass of brandy (optional)

1 tbsp sugar (if using brandy)

1 bottle of fruity, full bodied red wine chilled

1 orange thinly sliced, plus extra for garnish

1 lemon thinly sliced, plus extra for garnish

1 bottle of chilled Lemonade (2 litres)

To garnish:

A few fresh mint leaves and ice cubes

12 - 14 highball glasses

1. Put the orange juice and brandy (if using) in a pitcher. Stir in the sugar. When dissolved, add the wine, orange and lemon slices. This can be made the day before and kept in the fridge.
2. Just before serving, add the lemonade. Serve chilled over ice. Garnish with wafer thin slices of lemon, orange and a sprig of mint.

TIP:

*   For stronger sangria, use half the quantity of lemonade.

Punchy Pomegranate, Mint and Vodka

Serves 6

1 litre (1¾ pint) good quality pomegranate juice

Juice of 1 lime

Dash of vodka to taste

½ - 1 tsp peppermint extract, to taste

Crushed ice or ice cubes

To garnish:

A handful of fresh mint leaves

6 cocktail glasses

1. Mix the juices with vodka and peppermint.
2. Pour into glasses half filled with crushed ice, or couple of ice cubes and garnish.

Elderflower and Cassis Cordial

Serves 3 - 4

110 ml (4 fl oz) elderflower cordial, to taste

600 ml (1 pint) water, to taste

Dash of Crème de cassis, to taste

Juice of 1 - 2 fresh limes, to taste

To garnish:

A handful of blue borage flowers or fresh mint leaves with ice cubes

3 - 4 highball glasses

1. In a large jug mix the cordial, water, lime juice and dash of Cassis.
2. Pour into the glasses over ice and garnish.

Alcohol-Free Drinks

Home-made soft drinks are a lot more impressive, and are greatly appreciated by guests who do not drink alcohol. The ingredients are simple, demand very little of your time and they look chic.

TIP:

- Fresh juices on their own are not to everyone's taste. Some people find that drinking juices upsets their stomach, especially when they are made from highly acidic fruits like oranges. Try mixing fruit juices into these satisfying, non-alcoholic drinks.

Hot Spiced Apple Juice

This lovely drink is an alternative to mulled wine.

Serves 5 - 6

1 litre (1¾ pint) good quality apple juice

Zest of one orange

3 small cinnamon sticks cut in half

3 cloves

To garnish:

Wafer thin orange slices

5 - 6 small heatproof glasses

1. Place the apple juice and the rest of the ingredients in a large saucepan and heat gently over a low heat for about 10 minutes. Do not allow to boil. Then remove the cinnamon sticks.
2. Strain into a glass and garnish.

Cranberry & Elderflower Punch

This is a refreshing drink for every season. Delicious served hot or cold.

Serves 6

For a warm winter drink:

110 ml (4 fl oz) elderflower cordial, to taste

600 ml (1 pint) cranberry juice

600 ml (1 pint) water, to taste

To garnish:

A small handful of fresh or frozen and defrosted cranberries and a few sprigs of fresh mint

6 heatproof glasses

1. Place all the ingredients in a large saucepan and heat gently over a low heat for about 2 - 3 minutes - do not allow to boil.
2. Ladle into glasses and garnish.

For a cool summer drink:

Mix all the ingredients in a large jug. Serve chilled over ice and garnish.

Elderflower & Fresh Lime

Serves 4

165 ml (6 fl oz) elderflower cordial, to taste

600 ml (1 pint) water, to taste

Juice of 1 fresh lime, to taste

To garnish:

A handful of blue borage flowers or fresh mint leaves and ice cubes

4 highball glasses

1. In a large jug, mix the cordial, water and lime juice
2. Pour into the glasses over ice and garnish.

Refreshing Cordials

Any of these cordials will keep in the fridge for up to 3 days.

Cooling Lemonade

Serves 5

225 g (8 oz) caster sugar, to taste

Zest of one lemon

220 ml (8 fl oz) water for cooking

Fresh juice of 6 lemons

750 ml (1¼ pint) still or sparkling mineral water

Ice cubes

To garnish:

Slices of lemon and fresh mint leaves

5 highball glasses

1. Put the sugar, lemon zest and 250 ml water in a saucepan. Bring gently to the boil over a medium heat. Stir until the sugar is dissolved. Then add lemon juice and simmer for further 2 - 3 minutes. Leave to cool.
2. Pour into a jug and refrigerate.
3. Mix the syrup with chilled mineral water. Serve chilled over ice. Stir and garnish.

VARIATION

Lemonade with Saffron & Ginger

Take the above recipe and along with the rest of ingredients, add a small piece of fresh ginger root about 2 ½ cm (1 in) which has been peeled and sliced into the saucepan.

Discard the ginger early on if you want a mild flavour, or at the end of the cooking if you want more piquancy.

Add a small pinch of saffron to the lemon syrup after removing the saucepan from the heat. It gives the drink a beautiful light golden colour.

Note:

Even a little too much saffron will make the drink taste bitter.

Orange Cordial Scented with Lemon Grass

Serves 5 - 7

6 oranges

150 g (5 oz) granulated sugar

2 - 3 lemon grass stalks, stems bashed

Juice of 1 lemon

300 ml (½ pint) water for cooking

750 ml (1¼ pint) soda water, chilled

Ice cubes

To garnish:

One orange and 1 fresh lime, thinly sliced

5 - 7 highball glasses

1. Grate the zest from 2 oranges and then juice all the oranges.
2. Place the sugar, lemon grass and orange zest in a sauce pan with the water. Bring gently to the boil over a medium heat. Stir until the sugar dissolves, then simmer for about 5 minutes until it becomes syrupy. Allow to cool.
3. Then stir in the orange juice and lemon juice. Strain into a jug and refrigerate.

4. Place a couple of ice cubes in a glass, then half fill with orange cordial. Top up with soda water and stir.
5. Garnish each glass with a slice of orange on the rim.

Grape Juice with Cucumber & Black Olives

Serves 5 - 6

1 litre (1¾ pint) grape juice

5 black olives

1 small piece of cucumber cut into 5 diced cubes

5 - 6 cocktail sticks

Ice cubes

5 - 6 cocktail glasses

1. Skewer a piece of cucumber and olive on a cocktail stick.
2. Pour the juice over a couple of ice cubes in the glass and then place the skewer inside.

Tasty Apple Tonic

Serves 5 - 6

1 litre (1¾ pints) good quality apple juice

2½ cm (1 in) piece of fresh ginger, peeled and finely grated

Ice cubes

To garnish:

Wafer-thin red apple slices and few sprigs of fresh mint

5 - 6 highball glasses

Mix the apple juice and ginger. Serve chilled over ice and garnish.

Summer Cooler

A very refreshing drink for a hot summer day.

Serves 4

600 ml (1 pint) good quality orange juice

5 - 7 tsp runny honey, to taste

8 tbsp natural Greek yoghurt

Ice cubes

To garnish:

Few sprigs of fresh mint

4 highball glasses

1. Mix the juice, honey and yoghurt.
2. Pour the drink into the glasses filled with a couple of ice cubes and garnish.

Cheers!

Pre-Prepared Food for Drinks & Buffet Parties

Though nothing can replace a fine home-cooked meal, especially when you entertain, there are times when the last thing you want to do is slave away in a hot kitchen.

A quick visit to the nearest supermarket delicatessen to pick and mix may be just the answer to your entertainment woes.

Whether you offer a simple buffet, a cheese board or just some nibbles, time and effort is still a requisite for any meal. So it is worth selecting with care the best quality ingredients your budget will allow and make what you provide look inviting with personal touches, such as using attractive garnishes and serving on pretty plates. (As you may have seen at other parties, throwing nibbles in their packaging onto the table does very little to enhance the pleasure of eating them!).

To make your platter look elegant and enticing, pay attention to the colour and texture of your choices and be sure to mix in some appetizing bits and pieces.

TIP:

- You can keep costs low by using less meat and fewer cheeses and adding dips, crudities and a couple of interesting varieties of bread to your menu.

MENU IDEAS

Platters of:

- Dark pink prosciutto with peach-coloured cantaloupe
- Mixed salami with sun-dried tomatoes and roasted artichoke
- Buffalo mozzarella with baby tomatoes, fresh basil and olives
- Avocado dip or home-made guacamole - see page 69
- Crudities and bread sticks or home-made rosemary and garlic crostini - see page 74

ഔര

- A selection of enticing cold meats
- Hummus or home-made carrot and cucumber salsa - see page 162
- Tiny eggs hard boiled, served with a bowl of mayonnaise flavoured with fresh garlic and a pinch of mixed dried herb
- Wedges of cheese
- Chunks of good quality bread

ഔര

- Thinly sliced smoked chicken with lemon squeezed over
- Courgette or cucumber slices topped with Boursin or Roquefort cheese
- Sweet piquant peppers stuffed with feta cheese and walnut - see pages 80
- Couple of dips surrounded by crudities and bread sticks

For dessert serve:
A platter of fresh fruit or a couple of enticing puddings (see Puddings with Pizzazz)

Cheese and fruit platter

Cheese is a versatile food. With a glass of wine and some good accompaniments, it can make a lovely meal on its own.

A cheese and wine party is an informal, fun way to entertain friends and family.

Your Cheese Board – Homage to Fromage

At your party, the actual quantities of cheese and the additional accompaniments you offer will depend on whether your guests have eaten beforehand or if your offerings will replace the main meal.

TIPS:

- For a smaller gathering, it looks more impressive to serve two or three magnificent cheeses in huge chunks on the plate rather than dozens of tiny bits.
- For a larger party, offer 4 - 5 varieties of cheese.
- Make your cheese board interesting and attractive by selecting a wide variety. Ideally, a cheese board should offer one hard cheese, one soft creamy cheese to match with a powerful mature hard cheese, a goat's or sheep's milk variety as well as a ripe blue to your meal.
- Allow about 100 g (4 oz) cheese per person.
- If the cheese is served as part of the buffet with other desserts, then allow about 50 g (2 oz) per person.

Provide your guests with a small cheese plate or dessert plate with a small knife and fork.

Any of the following suggestions will complement your cheese board beautifully.

SUGGESTIONS:

- Serve one or a selection of crusty warm breads, pumpernickel, or a plate of oatcakes with fresh butter.
- A selection of apples and pears cut into wedges (lightly dipped in lemon juice), grapes, fresh figs, small chunks of cantaloupe and water melon, sliced cucumber or tomato, all work well with cheese.
- Use golden dried apricots, dates, figs, raisins, almonds and walnuts to garnish the cheese.
- Pickled walnuts or a little chutney are also good company on a cheese board.

If your wine and cheese party is going to be in place of dinner, consider serving the following:

A platter of enticing cold meats with some appetizing bits and pieces or some hot or cold canapés such as:

- Oven-baked honey and chilli sausages - see page 90
- Warm curried parsnip chips with a bowl of plain sour cream –see page 75
- Rosemary prawns and Parma ham skewers - see page 86
- Hummus with roasted pepper on garlic, herb crostini - see pages 73 and 74

For dessert, serve:

A platter of fresh fruit or a couple of enticing puddings (see Puddings with Pizzazz, page 168)

To enjoy your cheeses more, here are a few don'ts:

- Don't serve waxed cheese. To be credible, it needs a rind.
- Don't include any smoked cheeses - they affect the flavours of the other cheeses. If you are keen on smoked cheeses, make sure they are oak-smoked.
- Don't use the same knife to cut different cheeses - it will mix the flavours.
- Don't serve cheese with salted butter - it can dilute the taste of the cheese.
- Don't serve cheese straight from the fridge - allow it to reach room temperature.
- Don't store cheese in cling film - it lets moisture build up, encouraging mould. Instead, use waxed paper which allows the cheese to breathe but not to dry out.

> TIP:
> Whether a cheese course is served before or after dessert is a personal decision. If a good wine is served with the main course, cheese served before dessert offers a chance to finish the wine. The cheese in this case is eaten alone and is appreciated for its flavour and for the way it complements the wine

To store cheese

Some varieties of cheese are more perishable than others. For personal use, as a rule, buy all cheeses in small quantities at a time, especially soft cheeses such as Camembert and blue veined cheeses such as Roquefort. Hard or semi-hard cheeses will keep for days. They should be lightly wrapped in waxed paper or foil, put in a polythene bag and placed in the least cold part of the refrigerator. Take cheeses out about 1 hour before serving.

Wines to serve with cheeses

- Not all wines and cheeses enjoy an intimate relationship, and the type of cheeses you serve affects your choice of wine.
- Hard cheeses like Cheddar can work well with whites such as Chablis or Australian Chardonnay as well as reds like Chianti or Chilean Merlot. Cheddar served with tawny port is a great match.
- The flavour of Stilton is usually paired with port but also tastes delicious with sweet wines like Sauternes.
- The same is true for other blue cheeses such as the Shropshire blues and Roquefort. Partner creamy cheeses such as Brie, Camembert and goat's cheese with Sauvignon Blanc. If you want to drink dry red wine with cheese, choose a hard variety of cheese such as Manchego or Beaufort Comté.

> TIPS:
> - As a rough average, allow half a bottle of wine per head.
> - Supply some beer and cider for those guests who may prefer them.

Red chilli, bay leaves, carrots and olives

Glorious Garnishes

Presentation profoundly affects the way we perceive food. When it comes to food, colour and presentation are equally as important as taste. The sight of a beautiful dish stimulates our senses and boosts our eating pleasure because sharing a meal is much more than satisfying hunger. When you beautifully present your tasty offerings, this conveys the message, "*I care about you*". Garnishing a dish is fun and learning how to create mouth-watering temptations from ordinary food is an enjoyable experience.

TIPS:

- When placing the garnishes on the serving platters, balance is key. Place one large garnish in the centre with the food around it, or use a few garnishes as a decorative border.
- Elegant touches need not be costly and there are many ways to make any dish look beautiful: slivers of cucumber, batons of carrot, slices of lemon or lime, a sprig of lavender, a twig of shiny mint leaf, snow-white or rich-red rose petals, tiny clusters of bay leaves, feathery sprigs of rich green dill, red and green chillies, purple radishes, citrus fruit peel, a handful of berries, or crunchy ruby-coloured pomegranate seeds.
- While adding garnishes enhance dishes, keep in mind that less is always more. Use your imagination to move away from typical, rather boring garnishes. One sprig of chervil carefully positioned makes much more impact than an excess of parsley feathering the plate like an overgrown lawn.
- Garnishes can also become part of the recipe. A roast chicken surrounded with fresh sprigs of oregano and lemon slices needs nothing more. Neither does wafer-thin apple slices and orange segments overlapped in a semi-circle around a sponge cake. And a Chocolate, Almond and Pear Tart topped with fresh red currants looks great - page 184.
- Dishes with warm colours, like red and yellow, stimulate the appetite and bring a glow to the table.
- Colourful ingredients alone shine and don't need garnish. A plate of diced yellow pepper, cucumber, radishes, spring onion and grated carrots can be set off by pale green lettuce. Dress it with a light creamy vinaigrette dressing and you have a visual and gastronomic feast (page 165). But a simple dish of boiled potatoes may be livened up with a sprinkling of fresh chopped dill, chives or parsley.
- Have your garnishes ready in the fridge and use them at the last minute. (Wilted watercress and shrivelled lemons will make your guests wonder about the freshness of your food).

SUGGESTIONS:

- Just let your plate be your canvas. Be aware of colour as you dip into your own creative flair to bring interest to a dish with whatever is at hand, whether a few sprigs of mint from your garden, some black olives or a simple tomato and a bag of salad greens.

Flowers and food

Delicate edible flowers such as roses, pot marigolds (also known as calendula), nasturtiums, lavender, sweet violets, borage, dandelions, camomile, chives and thyme make an attractive and unusual garnish for many dishes. Also, adding a few petals to your salads and soups will make the dish more interesting and tasty.

TIP:

- Use only a few petals, otherwise they may overpower the flavour of your dish.

SUGGESTIONS:

- Scatter a few petals from a pretty purple thyme flower on pale green to make it more inviting. For example, on an Aromatic Spinach and Coconut Soup - see page 97.
- Use beautiful bright orange petals of pot marigolds in soups and stews or even rice for a lovely delicate flavour and a pleasant colour.
- Make a salad of ice-berg lettuce with a walnut dressing, more delicious and elegant with a few petals of nasturtium flowers, marigolds and dandelions.
- Add blue borage flowers to iced tea, gin and tonic or fruit punch.

Decorative garnishes from carving whole vegetables

Making these attractive garnishes is easy. You just need a good a knife and a little imagination to turn a humble red cabbage, an ordinary radish or lowly spring onions into a beautiful flower. Have fun, take your time and work carefully. This could make the difference between an uninspiring garnish and a successful, beautiful one.

If it's your first attempt at the art of food garnishing, it's is worth keeping in mind the following tips.

TIPS:

- Wash and dry all vegetables before carving.
- A good number of garnishes - such as carrots, celery, spring onion, leek, radish, cabbage, onion – after being carved need to be covered in cold water and refrigerated for a few hours to help vegetables become firm and to allow sliced sections to separate and curl.
- Most garnishes can be made a few days in advance.
- Prepared garnishes can be preserved up to a week. Cover them in cold water and store them in the fridge.

- Dip apple slices in lemon juice to prevent them from darkening. Lemon juice acts as a preservative when used to coat fruits and vegetables.

Radish fan

Make similar vertical slices down almost to the bottom of the radish but not right through it. It is easier to start in the middle and work outward. Cover the radishes with cold water - face down - and refrigerate for 3 - 4 hours - to open up the fan.

Radish Rose

Hold a radish with the stem end facing down. To form petals, make diagonal cuts close to the bottom and less than halfway into the radish. Cover in cold water - face down - and refrigerate for 3 - 4 hours to open up the petals.

Red cabbage flower

Use a sharp knife to make cuts half way into the cabbage and three-quarters of the way to the root end. Continue making these cuts evenly around the cabbage. Gently separate the layers and open up the flower. Cover in cold water - face down - and refrigerate for 3 - 5 hours, to open the petals further.

Spring onion flower

Trim away the root and most of the green stem, starting at 2 cm from the root end. Make 2 - 3 evenly spaced cuts into the centre and across the vegetable. Cover in cold water and refrigerate for 20 - 30 minutes to allow the petals to open and curl.

Interesting food containers

An unusual presentation will draw attention to your table. This is why hollowed-out bread loaves, large peppers, pumpkins, melon, water melon and pineapple make attractive food containers. They even reduce the washing up!

For an appetizing mix of colour, place them on a plate bordered with rich, green leaves. Fill the bread containers with nuts, dried fruit, bread sticks, or crisps. While the pretty vegetable containers can be filled with olives, crudities, dips and the fruit ones with a variety of juicy fruits respectively.

Hollowed bread filled with bread sticks and hollowed fruit filled with fruit

TIPS:

- Hollowed-out vegetables and fruit can be prepared up to two days ahead, covered and kept in the fridge ready for use.
- There is no waste when using hollowed-out vegetables as food servers. After use, they can be chopped and frozen for later use or added to stir-fries, soups or sauces.

To prepare:

Peppers and Pumpkins - Cut off the tops of the vegetables with a sharp knife and gently remove the seeds inside. To stop them from wobbling on the plate, cut a very thin slice from the bottom but please be careful as you don't want your filling to flow out of the cut underneath.

Melons and Pineapples - Cut the fruit in half and remove the flesh with a sharp knife. Dice the fruit and mix with contrasting coloured fruits - figs, apricots, nectarines, peaches, grapes, plums or berries. Pile them back inside the container.

Bread loaves - Fresh, soft bread loaf cut and hollowed will disintegrate too quickly, so your bread basket needs to be prepared in advance. You can cut and hollow the loaves up to 2 - 3 months ahead of time and dry them individually so that they don't lose their shape. Once dried, loaves can be stacked, covered with cling film and used several times.

With practice, it will become second nature to use whichever garnish you have readily available to turn, say, a casual supper into a special meal, and no matter how small your entertaining budget might be, your table can still look special and inviting.

Hollowed bread filled with grapes and dried fruit

Elements of Cooking

The first step to cooking a tasty meal does not start with the ingredients. It starts with reading through the recipe and various tips and getting a good sense of what the dish is about and then all the little touches which can help to enhance the food.

This will make it easier for you to vary recipes to suit your own personal preferences and to be able to spot the critical points in the recipe so that everything will come together and you will not be disappointed. For example, if you are using puff pastry in a dish or baking a cake, the critical point is the correct temperature of your oven. So knowing your own oven enables you to add an extra few minutes or turn the temperature down as necessary.

Use your own senses to help you judge things accurately and improvise. If, for example, the onions are not caramelizing properly, you may need to add another tablespoon of oil. Similarly, if the casserole is too watery, spoon the sauce into a pan and simmer uncovered until sufficiently reduced. Likewise, if the food tastes a bit bland, you can revive it by adding something of the following: a pinch of herbs, spices, chilli flakes or a bit of lemon / orange zest, a dash of lime juice, balsamic vinegar, or a tablespoon mayonnaise or Greek natural yoghurt.

The more cooking experience you have, the more you will be able to enhance your dishes by bringing the best out of your ingredients.

In cooking, you never stop learning.

The recipes in this section can be used and adapted to help you create a variety of colourful, tasty dishes for yourself and your guests.

Note: Oven temperatures in this book are for a conventional oven but if you have a fan oven then please reduce the temperature by 10 per cent.

GENERAL TIPS:

- When measuring ingredients make sure your scales are accurate. Incorrect weights can lead to disappointing results especially for cakes and puddings.
- Adding a little cream / natural yoghurt to soups, casseroles or hot sauces can improve their flavour. The most suitable in cooking are double cream, crème fraiche or Greek yoghurt. Their high fat content makes them very stable so they will not split when added to acidic ingredients when heated.
- To reduce any bitterness in a sauce, add salt, not sugar.
- If a casserole is too salty, add a couple of potatoes and cook for a few extra minutes but remove them before serving.
- Wash your utensils properly. There is nothing worse than eating a piece of fruit which has been cut with a knife that was also used for chopping garlic!
- Rub your hands with a slice of lemon to remove any onion or fish odours.

Nuts

Because of their high oil content, nuts can become rancid when exposed to air. To avoid this, carefully check the "use by" date. Once the pack is opened, seal tightly and store in the freezer or a dry place in a cupboard. Stale nuts taste bitter, disgusting and spoil the flavour of food.

Two suggestions for toasting nuts and seeds are as follows:

1. Place a non-stick frying pan over a high heat. Wait for a few seconds until it warms up. Then toss the nuts / seeds in the pan, reduce the heat to medium-low and stir for 2 - 3 minutes until lightly golden, then transfer into a bowl.
2. Spread the nuts / seeds in a single layer on a baking sheet and place in a pre-heated oven 190 °C / Gas mark 5. Toast for about 6 - 10 minutes (depending on the type of nuts used) and stir half way through to make sure they are evenly browned.

TIP:

*   The toasted nuts keep well for up to 3 - 4 days. Store at room temperature in an airtight container or freeze them and keep for up to one month.

Lemons, Limes and Oranges

I store lemons, limes and oranges in the fridge as this helps them last longer.

To zest: Use the fine side of a cheese grater and zest the citrus fruit over the dish so that you also capture the delicate mist of oil which is given out at the same time.

Take care not to include the white pith which will make the food bitter.

To produce the most juice, warm the citrus fruit to room temperature or heat them for a few second in the microwave then roll the whole fruit between your hands.

Chillies

Always wash your hands after handling chillies because they make your eyes sting if you happen to touch them.

TIP:

*   If too much chilli has been added to a dish then add half an un-squeezed lemon to help absorb the heat of the chilli.

Seasoning

Building and developing flavour at each step of cooking is the key to producing a tasty dish. Always lightly season vegetables with salt and pepper at the beginning of cooking. This helps to draw out some of the juices and infuses oil or butter with the aroma and flavour of the vegetables.

Saucepan Heat

Getting your pan to the right temperature is important as it helps to caramelise meat and vegetables to produce a tasty meal. At the correct temperature the oil will start to spread whereas in an under-heated pan, the oil stays in the middle and instead of browning the meat, it will heat slowly and stew in its own juices, causing you to end up with a tasteless piece of meat.

If the pan is too hot, the oil will start to discolour and spit and you could easily produce meat not properly cooked in the middle and with a bitter, burnt outer coating.

TIP:

- Heat the pan before adding oil and you will use less oil.

Browning Meat

Bring the meat to room temperature before cooking as cold meat may get too brown on the outside when it is cooked while the centre still remains undercooked.

To create a nicely coloured crust on the outside of the meat, it is important not to move the meat around whilst it is being browned. Leave it alone to cook. Bring your frying pan to a medium heat and add the oil. Once the oil starts to spread, swirl it around to coat the base of the pan evenly. Season the meat with salt and pepper and place flat in the pan. Remember do not do stir. Let a caramelized crust form, which will seal the meat and keeps it moist. After about 3 - 4 minutes, when the meat has browned on one side, turn it over and brown the other side.

Always brown meat in small batches - this is much quicker and avoids stewing the meat.

To Store Food

Food stored in the fridge must be properly protected as the refrigeration process draws out moisture.

TIPS:

- Food should be stored in a container or kept wrapped and covered in the fridge. This will help to keep the flavours of different foods from being absorbed into each other.
- Always wrap the food in kitchen foil or waxed paper (greaseproof paper is absorbent and not useful, as it allows evaporation to take place). Cling film can also be used to cover the surface of a dish to protect the food.

To Freeze Food

Freezing food is quite easy. For the best results, always make sure the food is cold before storing in the freezer. Wrap items such as salmon / chicken fillet or steaks individually in cling film and freeze on a tray, with each piece evenly spaced out. Never pile them in a bag, since this takes much longer to defrost and can even deform them.

Now to incorporate some of the elements of cooking into creating tasty foods and memorable occasions …

Oils

Olive oil

Extra virgin olive oil with its strong delicious taste and lovely dark green colour is more suitable for salad dressings and sauces than for frying as it burns easily at high temperatures. Blended olive oil with its mild flavour is good for both salad dressing and cooking.

> TIP:
>
> - Olive oil can become rancid when in contact with air, heat and light because the oxygen in the air reacts with chemicals in the oil. So store your oil in a cool dark place and not in a clear bottle by the stove. A rancid oil does not enhance the flavour of the salad.

Other oils

Vegetable oil is best for deep frying. Light oils such as sunflower, safflower, ground nut and cold pressed rapeseed are good for shallow frying and general cooking.

My favourites are the latter two. They have a nutty gentle flavour, do not overpower a dish and they act as a base on which to add more layers of flavour. Sesame oil with a low heating point burns quickly and should be saved for seasoning your dishes.

Flavoured oils

Using a drop of flavoured oil in your cooking or a salad dressing adds extra depth of flavour. It is very easy to make your own delicious herb oils.

You can use most herbs such as basil, tarragon, rosemary, parsley, chives or a mixture, for example, thyme and garlic.

Herbs should be washed and dried before use.

Here is a simple recipe:

Place about 30 g (1¼ oz) of fresh chopped herb with 150 ml (4 fl oz) oil in a liquidiser and blend until smooth. Then pour the oil into a small pan and heat very gently over a low heat for a few minutes until the colour changes to vibrant green. Cool and store in a glass bottle in the fridge for up to 3 - 4 days.

Herbs & Spices

Having a storage cupboard with a fair selection of herbs and spices allows you to add that wow-factor to your dish.

Herbs and spices play a big part in increasing the flavour of the food. Just remember they should be used sparingly - you want their flavours to enhance rather than overwhelm your cooking - sometimes a pinch too much can ruin the flavour of the dish.

TIP:

- Dried herbs and ground spices quickly lose their distinctive flavours within weeks of opening, so keep them stored in air-tight containers.

Herbs

Dried herbs are more concentrated than fresh herbs. Multiply the amount by four when using fresh herbs. For example, to season vegetables enough for 3 - 4 people, start with either 1 teaspoon of fresh herbs or ¼ teaspoon of dried herbs. Taste and add a little more if needed.

Some herbs, especially basil, rosemary, mint and chives should be chopped at the last minute as they quickly discolour. Wash and spin dry them before use.

Chopping also drastically reduces the volume of the herbs and releases their aromatic oil. For example, 1 tablespoon of chopped thyme will add a lot more flavour to a dish than a couple of sprigs of thyme.

As a guide, a 25 g (1 oz) pack of fresh herbs when chopped will yield around 4 tablespoons. The more mature the herb the stronger the flavour.

Chopped leftover fresh herbs can be frozen and used later in soups or casseroles. In order to freeze herbs, do the following:

1. Chop the herb, mix with couple of tablespoons of water and freeze in the ice cube tray.
2. Then tip the cubes into a freezer bag and store in the freezer for up to 1 month.

Also grated ginger, gravies and sauces can be frozen in a similar manner using the ice cube tray method but note that there is no need to add water.

Garlic

The way you prepare garlic affects the impact of its flavour in a dish. Crushing the clove will give a stronger taste than just chopping the clove.

Spices

The cinnamon, cardamom and ginger with their unique aromas and flavour make a dish more exotic. Do not be put off by some of the less common spices such as saffron, turmeric and smoked paprika. A touch of them greatly enhances the flavour of food. I have included them in a few recipes in this book. Once you get used to their unique flavour, there are many ways to use them in your everyday cooking.

Fresh ginger

Fresh gingerroot has a far more intense flavour than powdered ginger and it can be stored for a couple of weeks in the salad drawer of your fridge.

Cardamom

Cardamom adds a gentle fragrant flavour to a dish. It is most economical to buy cardamom in pods. Ground cardamom once opened loses its fragrance within few weeks.
To use cardamom: Wrap the pods in a small plastic bag and crush with a rolling pin. Remove the papery pods before sprinkling the crushed black seeds in a dish.

Saffron

Saffron with its golden colour and soft aroma can enliven many dishes. Saffron is not as expensive as it may seem. You only need a pinch of saffron to flavour a meal for 4 - 6 people. Crushing saffron threads before adding to a dish will help them to dissolve more quickly.

Turmeric

Turmeric can be used as an alternative to saffron. It gives a light golden colour but the flavour will not be the same as saffron.

Smoked paprika

Smoked paprika is also known as "Picante pimento". A touch of this spice gives a unique smoky flavour to dips, creamy salads, soups, casseroles, oven-baked salmon and particularly dishes with tomato sauce.
Note: The smoked paprika is produced by Bart and is available in Waitrose in the UK. Otherwise, check good supermarkets where you are.

TIP:

- Ground spices, such as turmeric and curry powder, should always be lightly cooked in a little oil before any liquid is added. This enhances their aroma and avoids a harsh raw taste.

Baba Ghanoush - smokey aubergine and yoghurt dip

Easy & Elegant Dips, Canapés & Light Bites

Dips, Canapés and home-made light bites add a personal touch to your party. You can offer a selection of inviting cocktail snacks on any budget. Attractive hors d'oeuvres are not just for sustenance. They create mood and can be a talking point.

This selection of tasty, colourful appetizers - some with a hint of a Middle Eastern accent - will add piquancy to your drinks and could also be a delicious way to introduce dinner. They are easy to prepare in advance and can be warmed through before eating.

Tips:

- Canapés should be easy to eat. Avoid foods that crumble or drip. If you are going to have a canapé-only party, offer at least four varieties. Depending on how light they are, allow 4 - 6 canapés per person for a 2 hour party and 7 - 10 per person if it is going to last longer, the last bit of which should be a sweet bite.
- If you are serving drinks and nibbles before a dinner or supper, 3 - 5 canapés per person will be plenty, keeping your main course and pudding in mind.
- Select the two best from your selection of hors d'oeuvres to wow your guests. Offer one at the beginning with drinks to warm up the atmosphere and the other at the end as something special, which will linger in your guests' memory.
- Place some of the hors d'oeuvres around the room on attractive platters. People tend to feel more relaxed if left to help themselves.
- In cooler weather serving a selection of hot and cold canapés is welcome.
- For a cocktail party that lasts more than 2 - 3 hours, it is appropriate to offer a mixture of 3 - 4 canapés, a couple of dips, crudities, cheese board and puddings.

Note:
Make sure there are serving spoons next to the dips and puddings, knives on the cheese platter and plenty of small plates, serviettes and forks available.

Dips

Dips are flavoursome, popular and simple to make.

Note:

Apart from Guacamole, dips can be prepared 1 - 2 days in advance and kept in the fridge. Left over dips are never wasted. They make delicious sauces for potatoes, vegetables, pasta, grilled fish or meat.

Guacamole

Serves 6 - 8

Vegetarian

4 medium tomatoes

3 ripe avocados (the Hass variety keeps its colour longer)

2 - 3 tbsp lemon juice or lime juice

2 garlic cloves, peeled and crushed

4 tbsp light crème fraiche or natural Greek yoghurt

½ small red onion or 3 spring onions trimmed and finely chopped

½ - 1 fresh red chilli, deseeded and finely chopped or a dash of hot chilli powder

1 tbsp fresh chopped coriander

Salt and black pepper

1. Cut the tomatoes in half, remove the seeds then finely chop the flesh.
2. Halve the avocados. Remove the stones but be sure to retain them (see Tip). With a teaspoon scrape off the avocado flesh and the remaining very green avocado flesh left clinging to the skin. (This is what gives the guacamole a really strong green colour). Add a dash of lemon juice to the avocado to delay browning.
3. Blend the avocados with lemon juice, crushed garlic and crème fraiche, in a blender, for a few seconds until creamy but not necessarily smooth. Alternatively mash the avocadoes with a fork almost to a purée before adding the rest of the ingredients.
4. Spoon into a bowl and add the onion, chilli, coriander and tomatoes. Taste and season. Cover and store in the fridge - see Tip below.
5. Give it a good stir before serving.

Note:

For a cooler taste, leave out the chilli.

VARIATION

Leave out the crème fraiche or natural Greek yoghurt and onion and replace the chilli with a dash of Tabasco sauce.

TIP:

To delay the Guacamole discolouring and help it stay green for 6 - 8 hours:
- Always use ripe avocados.
- Place a couple of avocado stones into the dip when storing in the fridge. Remember to remove the stones before taking to the table.
- To prevent air reaching the Guacamole, tightly cover the dish with cling film and carefully press it to touch the surface of the dip.

Spinach & Pan Roasted Red Onion with Yoghurt

Serves 7 - 9
Vegetarian

3 tbsp olive oil
1 medium red onion, peeled and finely chopped
2 garlic cloves, peeled and crushed
½ tsp ground turmeric
200 g (7 oz) fresh spinach washed, pat dried and roughly chopped

1 x 500 g tub natural Greek yoghurt or light crème fraiche
1 - 2 tbsp light mayonnaise
Dash of lemon or lime juice (optional)
Salt and pepper
Handful of roughly chopped walnuts (optional)

1. Heat the oil in a non-stick frying pan. Add the onion and sauté over a medium heat until soft and lightly golden. Sprinkle over the crushed garlic and turmeric and cook for 30 - 40 seconds. Then add the spinach and cook over a high heat for 3 - 4 minutes until wilted. Remove from the heat and let cool.
2. Place the spinach and yoghurt in a food processor and whiz for a few seconds until roughly smooth.
3. Transfer into a bowl. Mix in the mayonnaise and lemon juice. Season to taste. Cover and refrigerate. If using walnuts, stir them in just before serving.

Baba Ghanoush - Smokey Aubergine & Yoghurt Dip

This dip with its delicious smokey taste makes a good accompaniment to grilled lamb or beef. Here are three of my favourite recipes for this dip:

Serves 7 - 9
Vegetarian

3 medium seedless aubergines, about 700 g (1½ lb)
4 tbsp olive oil
1 medium red onion, peeled and finely chopped
3 garlic cloves, peeled and crushed

½ tsp ground turmeric or a pinch of ground saffron or saffron threads
5 - 6 tbsp natural Greek yoghurt or light crème fraiche
Dash of lemon juice

| 1 tsp dried mint or 1 tbsp chopped fresh mint | Handful of roughly chopped walnuts (optional) |

1. Pre-heat the oven to 200 °C / 400 °F / Gas mark 6.
2. Wash the aubergines, pat dry and halve vertically. Rub the surface with lemon juice to prevent discolouration. Prick all over the flesh with a fork - careful not to pierce the skin. Then brush the aubergines lightly with 1 tablespoon of oil and place on an oven tray - flesh side up.
3. Bake for about 50 minutes or until soft and golden brown. Then remove from the oven and let cool. Scoop out the soft flesh from the skins and remove any seeds.
4. Meanwhile heat the remaining 3 tablespoons of oil in a non-stick frying pan. Add the onion and sauté over a medium heat until soft and lightly golden. Stir in the garlic and turmeric and cook for 30 - 40 seconds. Then add the aubergines and saffron, if using. Mix well, cover and cook over a low heat for another 5 minutes. Remove from the heat and allow to cool.
5. Place the aubergine mixture, yoghurt and lime juice in a food processor and blend for a few seconds until smooth.

Transfer into a bowl and add the mint walnuts, if using.

If the dip is too thick, add a couple of spoonfuls of yoghurt. Season to taste.

Variation

Smokey Aubergine & Hummus Dip

Prepare the aubergines to the end of step 3. Place in a blender with 4 - 5 tablespoons of ready-made hummus and a dash of lemon juice. Blend until smooth.

Transfer into a bowl. Season to taste. Stir in 1 - 2 tablespoons of fresh chopped coriander (optional).

Persian Style Mint Yoghurt

This light, refreshing dip is also a good accompaniment to Spicy Roast Potato Wedges or Curried Parsnip Chips - see pages 76, 75.

Serves 6 - 8

Vegetarian

1 x 500 g tub natural Greek yoghurt	
1 garlic clove, peeled and crushed	2 - 3 tbsp mayonnaise
1 - 1½ tbsp freshly chopped mint or ½ tsp dried mint	Salt and pepper

Mix together all the ingredients. Season to taste.

Dips That can also be Served as Canapés

In these recipes the thickness of the mixture makes them suitable for spreading.

To serve as Canapés:

a) spread them over fine slices of courgettes, cucumber, or

b) serve on crispy bread, crostini, or oven roasted baby potatoes - see pages 74 and 77.

To serve as a dip, just add 5 - 7 tablespoons of crème fraiche or natural Greek yoghurt to the mixture.

Oven Roasted Red Pepper, Red Onion & Feta Cheese

Makes 20 - 25 canapés

Serves 7 - 9 as a dip

Vegetarian

3 tbsp olive oil

1 red pepper, deseeded and cut into small chunks

1 small red onion, peeled and roughly chopped

200 g (7 oz) feta cheese, finely crumbled

1 - 2 tbsp light crème fraiche or natural Greek yoghurt

½ tsp dried oregano or mixed herbs

Dash of lemon juice (optional)

Salt and pepper

1. Pre-heat the oven to 200 °C / 400 °F / Gas mark 6.
2. Heat the oil in a large roasting tin. Then add the pepper and onion, lightly season with salt and pepper and toss to coat. Roast in the oven for 20 - 25 minutes or until soft and golden. Remove from the oven and let cool.
3. Place the vegetables with their juices from the tin, along with the cheese, yoghurt and herbs in a food processor and blend for a few seconds until smooth.
4. Transfer into a dish. Taste and adjust the seasoning. Add a dash of lemon juice, if required. Serve on thin slices of courgettes or cucumber.

Note:

The dip thickens up after being stored in the fridge for several hours. Before spreading, you may need to add another tablespoon of yoghurt to it.

Aduki (Azuki) Beans Hummus

This delicious Hummus can also be made with Pinto or Borlotti beans.

Makes 16 - 18 canapés

Serves 4 - 5 as a dip

Vegetarian

1 x 400 g tin of Aduki beans, drained and rinsed or 125 g (5 oz) of dried beans, soaked and cooked - see page 138.

4 tbsp olive oil

1 medium red onion, peeled and finely chopped

3 garlic cloves, peeled, and crushed

2 - 2½ tbsp tomato purée, to taste

½ tsp ground cumin

½ tsp hot chilli powder or ½ - 1 fresh
  red chilli, deseeded and finely
  chopped, to taste

2 - 3 tsp lemon juice

3 tbsp water

1 large tomato, deseeded and finely
  chopped

3 spring onions, trimmed and finely
  chopped

Salt

1. Heat the oil in a frying pan and sauté the onion over a medium heat until soft and
   golden. Add the garlic and cook for 30 - 35 seconds before stirring in the beans, tomato
   purée, spices, lemon juice and water. Lightly season with salt. Cover and simmer over a
   low heat for about 5 minutes for beans to absorb the flavours. Remove from the heat.
   Cool.

2. Blend the mixture in a food processor until smooth.

3. Transfer into a dish. If the bean hummus is going to be used as a dip, add 1 - 2
   tablespoons of water to the paste before adding the tomato and spring onions.
   Season to taste.

Hummus with Roasted Pepper

To serve as a dip, you may need to add more olive oil to the mixture in these two Hummus
recipes.

Makes 20 canapés

Serves 5 - 7 as a dip

Vegetarian

1 x 400 g tin of chickpeas, drained and
  rinsed or 125 g (5 oz) of dried beans,
  soaked and cooked - see page 138.

3 tbsp olive oil

2 red peppers, deseeded and cut into
  small chunks

2 garlic cloves, peeled and finely crushed

Juice of 1 - 1½ lemon

2 - 3 tbsp tahini (see Note following)

Salt and pepper

1. Pre-heat the oven to 200 °C / 400 °F / Gas mark 6.

2. Heat the oil in a large roasting tin. Add the peppers, lightly season with and pepper and
   toss to coat. Roast for 15 - 20 minutes or until soft and golden. Remove from the oven.

3. Toss in the chick peas and stir until they are coated with the seasoned oil. Let cool.

4. Place the mixture with the garlic, lemon juice and tahini in a food processor and blend
   until smooth. Add a drizzle of olive oil to loosen, if needed.

5. Transfer into a bowl. Season to taste.

Plain Hummus

Serves 4

Leave out the red peppers and just blend all the ingredients in a food processor. You may need to add a bit more olive oil, lemon juice and tahini and a dash of cayenne pepper is optional.
Note: Tahini is made from crushed roasted sesame seeds blended with sesame oil.

Delicious Dipping Sticks

Garlic, Herb Crostini

The Italian word crostini means little toasts, i.e. a piece of thin, crispy toast.
When cooled, these crostinis will keep for up to 1 day in an airtight container.
Makes 30 - 35

1 large fresh thin baguette, sliced, about 1¼ cm (½ in) thick	2 garlic cloves, peeled and crushed
3 tbsp olive oil	1 tsp dried herbs

1. Pre-heat the oven to 180 °C / 350 °F / Gas mark 4.
2. In a small bowl, mix the oil, garlic and herb. Then spread all over a large baking tray.
3. Next lay the bread slices on the tray and then turn each one over so that both sides have been lightly coated with the flavoured oil.
4. Bake in the oven for about 10 minutes or until lightly golden. (Keep an eye on them because 1 - 2 minutes too long and they may burn).

Garlic, Herb, Parmesan Cheese Crostini

After coating the bread with the flavoured oil, dust the slices with parmesan cheese and then continue to follow the recipe.

Rosemary & Garlic Crostini

When cooled, these crostinis keep well for up to 2 days in an airtight container. If you wish to serve the crostinis warm, place them on an oven tray and reheat in a pre-heated oven (180 °C / 350 °F / Gas mark 4) for 2 - 3 minutes.
Makes 30 - 35

1 large fresh thin baguette, sliced about 1¼ cm (½ in) thick	150 g (6 oz) butter
1 tbsp dried rosemary	4 garlic cloves, peeled and crushed

1. Pre-heat the oven to 200 °C / 400 °F / Gas mark 6.
2. Melt the butter in a small saucepan on a low heat, add the garlic and rosemary. Remove from the heat.
3. Spread each slice of bread with the flavoured butter, then place on a baking tray and cook for 5 minutes or until golden.

Roasted Sesame Pitta Wedges

These tasty pitta wedges can be prepared 5 - 6 hours in advance. If you want to serve them warm, spread the wedges out on a large roasting tray and warm through in a pre-heated oven (190 °C / 380 °F / Gas mark 5) for 1 - 2 minutes. Be careful - they can burn easily!
Makes 24 wedges

6 white pitta bread

4 - 6 tbsp olive oil

1½ tbsp dried thyme, mixed herbs or
   rosemary

1 tsp paprika

2½ tbsp toasted sesame seeds

1. Pre-heat the oven to 200 °C / 400 °F / Gas mark 6.
2. In a bowl, combine the oil, herb and paprika.
3. Place the pitta bread on a cutting board and brush lightly with the flavoured oil. Then sprinkle over the sesame seeds.
4. Cut the bread into wedges and carefully lay them on a large baking tray.
5. Cook in the oven for 4 - 5 minutes or until lightly golden.

VARIATION

Roasted Garlic Pitta Wedges

Leave out the sesame seeds, herbs and paprika. Cut a big garlic clove in half and rub over the pitta bread before brushing with the olive oil. Sprinkle with a touch of cayenne pepper. Then follow the recipe as shown above, starting from step 3.

Curried Parsnip Chips

These appetizing chips could be prepared up to 3 - 4 hours in advance and served at room temperature.
Makes 35 - 40
Vegetarian

700 g (1½ lb) parsnips washed, peeled
   and cut into chips roughly 5 x 2½
   cm (2 x 1 in) thick

4 tbsp olive oil

1 - 1½ tsp curry powder or Balti curry
   paste

2 tbsp chopped parsley

Salt and pepper

To garnish:

Parsley

1. Pre-heat oven to 200 °C / 400 °F / Gas mark 6.
2. In a large bowl, mix the oil and curry powder or curry paste. Add the parsnips, lightly season with salt and pepper and toss to coat.
3. Then spread the parsnips out on a large roasting tray and roast in the oven for 25 - 30 minutes or until lightly golden and soft. Remove from the oven.
4. Serve with a bowl of plain sour cream or Persian style mint yoghurt (page 71) and cocktail sticks to spear.

Prepare ahead:

The roasted parsnip chips keep well in the fridge for up to 1 day.

To use:

Either warm through in a pre-heated oven (200 °C / 400 °F / Gas mark 6) for 3 - 5 minutes, or briefly warm in a microwave for 1 - 2 minutes.

Gently Spiced Roast Potato Wedges

Makes 32 - 35

Vegetarian

4 large potatoes about 250 g (10 oz) each (such as King Edward or Maris Piper), washed and pat dried	½ tsp smoked paprika, or hot chilli powder
5 - 6 tbsp olive oil	1 tsp paprika
	1 tbsp cumin
	1½ tsp salt

1. Pre-heat the oven to 200 °C / 400 °F / Gas mark 6.
2. Cut the potatoes into chips roughly 5 x 2½ cm (2 x 1in) thick, skins left on.
3. In a large bowl, combine the oil, smoked paprika or chilli powder, paprika, cumin and salt. Add the potatoes and toss to coat.
4. Spread the potatoes out on a large roasting tray, and roast in the oven for 25 - 30 minutes or until lightly golden and soft.
5. Serve with a refreshing dip such as sour cream flavoured with chives or Persian style mint yoghurt or plain hummus (see pages 71, 74) and cocktail sticks to spear.

Prepare ahead:

Roast the potatoes for up to 4 - 5 hours in advance. When ready to serve, either warm the potatoes through in a pre-heated oven (200 °C / 400 °F / Gas mark 6) for 5 - 7 minutes, or briefly warm in a microwave for 1 - 2 minutes.

Rosemary & Garlic Roast Potato Wedges

Leave out the cumin and smoked paprika or hot chilli powder. Add 1½ teaspoons of dried rosemary and 2 garlic cloves, peeled and crushed, to the olive oil. Then follow the recipe.

Oven Roasted Baby Potatoes

These potatoes bites are also delicious when topped with Horseradish Beef Fillet - see recipe on page 93.

Makes about 36

Vegetarian

18 small new potatoes, washed, pat dried, unpeeled, and halved lengthways (see Tip below)

3 - 4 tbsp olive oil

½ tsp dried rosemary
1 - 2 garlic cloves, peeled and crushed
Salt and pepper

1. Pre-heat the oven to 200 °C / 400 °F / Gas mark 6.
2. In large bowl combine the olive oil, garlic and rosemary. Add the potatoes, lightly season them with salt and pepper, then toss to coat.
3. Spread the potatoes out in a large roasting tin. Roast for 20 - 25 minutes or until golden and softened, turning over half way through cooking. Remove from the oven.
4. Serve with a refreshing dip such as sour cream flavoured with chives or spinach and pan-roasted red onions with yoghurt (see page 70) and cocktail sticks to spear.

TIP:

• If the baby potatoes are going to be used for Horseradish Beef Fillet or spreading with the canapé topping, then it is best to:

❧ Before cutting the potatoes in half, slice a fine sliver off both sides to stop them from wobbling on the plate.

❧ Let the potatoes cool slightly before use.

Prepare ahead:
Roasted potatoes keep well in the fridge for up to 2 days.

To use:
Either place the potatoes uncovered on a baking tray then place in a warm oven (180 °C / 350 °F / Gas mark 4) for 6 - 8 minutes to lightly crisp up. Or briefly warm in a microwave for 1 - 2 minutes.

Tɪᴘ:

- Always spread oat cakes and crisp breads with a thin layer of butter before using as a canapé base. This will keep your canapés crisp and prevents sogginess from the topping.

Mini Oat Cakes with Smoked Salmon & Lumpfish Caviar

Makes about 40

About 150 ml (5 fl oz) crème fraiche

4 spring onions, trimmed and finely chopped

40 mini oat cakes, spread lightly with butter

350 g (10 oz) smoked salmon

1 x 100 g (4 oz) jar Lumpfish red caviar (see Note below)

Ground black pepper

1. Mix the crème fraiche with spring onions and season with black pepper.
2. Slice the salmon into bite-size slivers and place on the oatcake.
3. Top the canapé with a teaspoonful of crème fraiche mixture and sprinkle with the caviar.

Note:
Lumpfish red caviar is available in Waitrose and a few other good supermarkets.

Prepare ahead:
The crème fraiche prepared at step 1 will keep in the fridge for up to 2 days. Prepare the canapés to the end of step 2 three hours in advance, cover loosely and refrigerate. An hour before serving, remove from the fridge and top with the crème fraiche and caviar.

Salmon, Crème Fraiche & Horseradish with Crostini

Makes about 20 - 25
For the crostini:
1 large fresh thin baguette, finely sliced, about 1¼ cm (½ in) thick

For the pâté:

1 x 180 g tin of skinless and boneless salmon, well drained

1 tbsp crème fraiche

Dash of lemon juice

Salt and pepper

1 tbsp jarred horseradish sauce, to taste

2 - 3 spring onions, trimmed and finely chopped

Knob of butter at room temperature

To garnish:

Use slivers of cucumber and radish or a handful of rocket.

1. Pre-heat the grill to hot and toast the slices of baguette on both sides until golden. Cool.
2. Roughly flake the salmon. Mix with the crème fraiche, horseradish and a dash of lemon juice. If the pâté is too dry, add another ½ - 1 tablespoon of crème fraiche. Then stir in the spring onions and season to taste.
3. Lightly spread the crostini with butter, top with a spoon full of pâté and garnish.

Note:

You may replace the Crostini with thinly sliced courgette.

Smoked Rainbow Trout with chives on Pumpernickel

Makes 20 - 25

250 g (10 oz) smoked rainbow trout fillet

4 tbsp light crème fraiche

Dash of cayenne pepper

1 tbsp chopped fresh chives or 2 spring onions, trimmed and finely chopped

Dash of lemon juice (optional)

Freshly ground black pepper

5 slices of pumpernickel bread, spread lightly with butter

1. Roughly chop the trout fillet and place in a food processor with crème fraiche and cayenne pepper. Blend until smooth. Transfer into a bowl. If the pâté is too dry, add another ½ - 1 tablespoon of crème fraiche. Then stir in the chives or spring onions. Taste and adjust seasoning.
2. Cut the bread into bite-size rectangles, top with a spoon full of pâté and garnish.

Note:

You may replace pumpernickel with thinly sliced courgette.

Colourful, Simple & Refreshing Nibbles

Marinated Olives

A selection of olives is always a welcome addition to any party. You can make your own flavoured olives. These marinated olives keep well in the fridge for up to 1 - 2 weeks

Serves 8 - 10

1x 350 g (12 oz) jar of pitted green or black olives, drained

½ tsp dried oregano, thyme or mixed herbs

2 garlic cloves, peeled and crushed

½ tsp cumin

½ fresh red chilli, deseeded and finely chopped

3 - 4 tbsp olive oil

Mix the olives with the rest of the ingredients in a bowl. Cover and store in a cool place for 2 - 3 days to absorb the flavours. Stir the olives occasionally.

VARIATION

Replace the cumin and herbs with 1 tablespoon of finely chopped fresh parsley as well as the grated zest of a lemon.

These tasty light bites keep well in a cool place for up to 3 hours.

Mini Tomatoes Sandwiches with Mozzarella & Basil

Serves 20

Vegetarian

125 g (5 oz) mozzarella cheese

20 baby cherry tomatoes

20 basil leaves

20 cocktail stick

1. Cut the mozzarella into very thin slices, about ½ x ½ cm (¼ x ¼ in)
2. Cut the baby tomatoes in half horizontally. Sandwich together the tomato halves with slices of mozzarella and basil leaves. Secure with a cocktail stick.

Sweet Piquante Peppers Stuffed with Feta Cheese, Walnut or Pecan Nuts

Makes about 28 - 30

Vegetarian

1 jar of mild Peppadew (see Note below)

200 g (7 oz) of finely sliced feta cheese

28 - 30 small pieces of walnuts or pecan nuts

Few sprigs of fresh mint

1. Drain and empty the jar in a colander. Then stuff each pepper with a couple of slices of feta cheese and a piece of walnut or pecan nut.
2. Scatter over the fresh mint before taking to the table.

Note:

The piquante peppers that are too tiny to be filled can make a delicious addition to salads - see page 161.

Jars of Peppadew are available in most good supermarkets.

Cucumber / Courgette with Garlic & Herb Boursin

Makes 20 - 22
Vegetarian

1 x 150 g (6 oz) garlic and herb Boursin
1 tbsp crème fraiche or natural Greek
  yoghurt
Pinch of salt

1 large cucumber or 2 medium
  courgettes thinly sliced, about 2½ cm
  (1 in) thick

To garnish:

Slivers of radishes or chopped chives

1. Place the Boursin in a bowl and mash with a fork. Add the crème fraiche or yoghurt to give it a thick consistency - if required, add a little more. Taste and adjust the seasoning.
2. Top each cucumber slice or courgette with a teaspoonful of cheese mixture and garnish.

TIPS:

- You may substitute the Boursin with 200 g (7 oz) plain cream cheese which has been mixed with 1 - 2 crushed garlic cloves, ½ teaspoon dried thyme (or mixed herbs), a dash of lemon juice and a pinch of salt.

Prepare ahead:

The Boursin prepared in step 1 or the cream cheese substitute keep well in the fridge for up to 2 days.

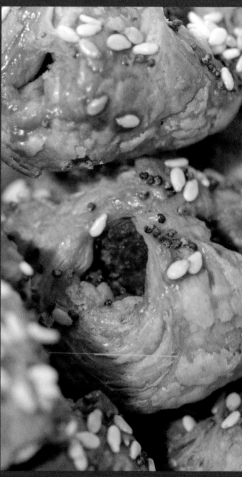

Chorizo puffs

Tasty Mini Puffs

These are ideal finger foods to serve with drinks, easy to make and can be prepared in advance. Here are three of my favourite recipes.

Boursin Cheese Puffs with Sesame & Poppy Seeds

Makes about 18 - 20

Vegetarian

Flour for dusting

1 x 375 g (13 oz) pack pre-rolled puff pastry

1 x 150 g (6 oz) garlic and herb Boursin

1 egg to glaze

1 - 2 tbsp each of sesame and poppy seeds

1. Dust the work surface with flour. Unroll the sheet of puff pastry and cut into tiny squares about 5x5 cm. (2x2 in) Then place a generous teaspoonful of Boursin in the centre of each square. Fold over to form a crescent or a cube shape. Pinch the edges together, taking care not to squeeze out the filling. Chill for one hour.
2. Pre-heat oven to 220 °C / 425 °F / Gas mark 7.
3. Beat the egg and lightly brush over each piece. Gently prick the pastry top with a fork. Then sprinkle generously with sesame and poppy seeds.
4. Cover a baking tray with baking parchment and place the pastries on it. Cook for 8 - 10 minutes or until risen and golden. Immediately remove from the tray and cool on a wire rack.

Chorizo Puffs

Makes about 18 - 20

Here the Boursin is replaced with 125 g (5 oz) of finely chopped spicy chorizo or pepperoni sausages.

To prepare and cook, follow the same instructions as for Boursin puffs with sesame and poppy seeds.

Prepare ahead:

You may use either of these TWO options:

1. Prepare the pastries up to the end of step 1, cover and store in the fridge for up to 1 day. When ready to use, carry on from step 2.
2. Cook the Boursin or chorizo puffs one day in advance. Then store them in an air tight container and refrigerate. You may serve the pasties at room temperature or reheat them on a baking tray, uncovered, in a pre-heated oven (200 °C / 400 °F / Gas mark 6) for 1 - 2 minutes.

Potato & Parsnip Rosti

with goat's cheese, cranberry marmalade & pistachio

Rostis are a type of pancake mostly made from potatoes. These delicious rostis can be assembled an hour or two before serving.

Makes 20 - 25

Vegetarian

For the marmalade:
1½ tbsp sugar

2 tbsp water

150 g (6 oz) fresh or frozen and defrosted cranberries

100 ml (4 fl oz) orange juice

Grated zest of 1 orange

Rosti with cranberries

For the rosti:
250 g (10 oz) potatoes, peeled and grated

150 g (6 oz) parsnips, peeled and grated

1 small red onion, peeled and finely chopped

2 eggs lightly beaten

Salt and pepper

3 - 4 tbsp oil for frying

For the base:
Mini oat cakes or Garlic, herb Crostini - see page 74.

For the topping:
100 g (4 oz) goat cheese finely sliced

To garnish:
50 g (2 oz) chopped pistachio, or sprigs of fresh mint.

1. First make the marmalade. In a small pan, dissolve the sugar in the water over a low heat. Add the cranberries, orange juice and orange zest and simmer gently for 4 - 5 minutes. Stir occasionally until the cranberries start to burst but are not mushy. The mixture will be slightly thickened. Remove from the heat and cool.

2. Then make the rosti. Place the grated potatoes and parsnip in a colander and squeeze out the moisture. Then tip into a large bowl. Add the onion and eggs to the mixture and lightly season with salt and pepper.

3. Heat the oil in a non–stick frying pan. Add full teaspoonful of potato mixture (1 full teaspoonful of the mixture for each rosti). Cook over a medium heat in small batches for 2 - 3 minutes on each side until golden and crisp. Drain on kitchen paper.

4. When ready to serve, place a rosti on an oat cake or garlic, herb crostini. Top with a slice of goat cheese and a teaspoonful of cranberry sauce.

Prepare ahead:

The cranberry marmalade will keep in the fridge for up to one week.

The rosti will keep in the fridge for up to 3 days and freeze well.

To freeze:

Cover a large plate with waxed paper. Place the cool rostis in a single layer on the plate. Lay another piece of waxed paper on top of the rostis and repeat the process until all rostis have been used. Wrap the plate fully with waxed paper then place in a freezer bag and freeze.

To use:

Place the frozen rostis on a baking sheet and reheat in a pre-heated oven (200 °C / 400 °F / Gas mark 6) for 6 - 8 minutes.

Alternatively, thaw the rostis overnight in the fridge or leave out in your kitchen to defrost for about 2 - 3 hours. Reheat slightly in a pre-heated oven (200 °C / 400 °F / Gas mark 6) for 2 - 3 minutes before carrying out step 4.

Gently Spiced Prawns with Mango Chutney Yoghurt Dip

After grilling these prawns keep well for up to 1 day in the fridge. Serve at room temperature.

Makes 20 skewers

    40 raw fresh or frozen and defrosted
       peeled prawns

For the marinade:

    2½ cm (1 in) piece of fresh ginger,
       peeled and grated (about 1 tsp)
    1 tbsp olive oil
    1 tbsp light soy sauce
    2 garlic cloves, peeled and crushed
    Juice of 1 lime

For the dip:

    7 tbsp natural Greek yoghurt   1½ tbsp spiced mango chutney

20 cocktails sticks soaked in cold water for 30 - 40 minutes to prevent burning during cooking.

1. In a large bowl combine all the ingredients for the marinade.
2. Then add the prawns, and turn to coat in the marinade. Cover and store in a cool place for 2 - 3 hours or overnight in the fridge.

3. Meanwhile, prepare the dip. Mix the yoghurt and mango chutney in a small bowl. Cover and store in a cool place.
4. Turn on your grill to maximum.
5. Thread 2 prawns onto a cocktail stick
6. Then cook the prawns under the hot grill for 3 - 4 minutes on each side or until the prawns are firm, turning once
7. Serve with the mango chutney yoghurt dip.

Prepare ahead:
Complete to the end of step 3, one day in advance. Cover and refrigerate.

To use:
Continue the recipe from step 4.

Rosemary Prawns & Parma Ham Skewers

After grilling these prawns keep well for up to 1 day in the fridge. Serve at room temperature. They are also great for a buffet and make a lovely light main course (see suggestion on page 105). Makes 24 skewers

12 Parma ham slices cut in half
24 raw fresh or frozen and defrosted peeled prawns

For the marinade:

1 tsp paprika

1 tsp rosemary

5 tbsp olive oil

3 garlic cloves, peeled and crushed

To garnish:
Two limes cut into small wedges.

1. Soak 24 cocktails sticks in cold water for 30 - 40 minutes to prevent burning during cooking.
2. In a large bowl, combine all the ingredients for marinade.
3. Then add the prawns, and turn to coat in the marinade. Cover and store in a cool place for 2 - 3 hours or overnight in the fridge.
4. Wrap each prawn in half a piece of Parma ham.
5. Thread one prawn onto a cocktail stick
6. Turn on your grill to maximum.
7. Then cook the prawns under the hot grill for 3 - 5 minutes on each side or until the prawns are firm, turning once.
8. Place the prawn skewers on a large white platter and garnish with 2 limes cut into small wedges.

Prepare ahead:

Complete to the end of step 3, one day in advance. Cover and refrigerate.

To use:

Continue the recipe from step 4.

Persian Style Chicken Kebab

The marriage of orange zest, saffron and yoghurt makes a delicious marinade for this chicken kebab. You may grill the chicken 2 - 3 hours in advance and serve at room temperature. Serve with Persian Style Mint yoghurt (see page 71) and cocktail sticks to spear.

These kebabs make a lovely platter for a buffet party.

Makes 24 - 26

    4 chicken breast fillets, about 600 g (1 lb 5 oz)

    Salt and pepper

For the marinade:

    1 large red onion, peeled and finely chopped

    1 tsp saffron threads, crushed or a pinch of ground saffron

    3 tbsp olive oil

    Juice of 1 lime

    Zest of 1 small orange

    2 - 3 fat garlic cloves, peeled and crushed

    3 tbsp natural Greek yoghurt

1. Cut the chicken into 2½ cm (1 in) cubes, and lightly season with salt and pepper.
2. In a large bowl, combine all the ingredients for the marinade.
3. Add the chicken pieces and turn to coat in the marinade - score the surface of the chicken pieces with the tip of a sharp kitchen knife a few times to allow the meat absorb the flavour. Cover and store in a cool place for 2 - 3 hours or overnight in the fridge. Turn the chicken in the marinade a couple of times during this period.
4. Turn on your grill to maximum.
5. Place the chicken pieces in a single layer in a shallow oven tray. Cook under the hot grill for 8 - 10 minutes on each side or until cooked all the way through.

Prepare ahead:

The grilled chicken will keep in the fridge for up to 1 day. It also tastes delicious if served cold.

To use:

If you want to reheat the chicken here are 3 options:

A:

Briefly warm in a microwave for 1 - 2 minutes.

B:

Melt a knob of butter about 12 g (½ oz) with 2 tbsp of water.

Place the chicken pieces on a roasting tray and baste with the butter mixture.

Then heat through uncovered in a pre-heated oven (200 °C / 400 °F / Gas mark 6) for 2 - 3 minutes, turning the chicken over, baste and heat for another 2 - 3 minutes.

C:

In a large non-stick frying pan melt the butter with the water over a medium-low heat.

Add the chicken pieces, cover with a lid, and heat through for 1 - 2 minutes on each side.

Lightly Spiced grilled Chicken Bites

You can also make a delicious warm salad with this chicken - see recipe page 118.

Makes 20 - 22

> 4 chicken breast fillets, about 600 g (1 lb 5 oz)

For the marinade:

1½ tbsp Balti curry paste	2 tbsp mild olive oil
1½ tbsp spiced mango chutney	3 tbsp white wine or cider vinegar
2 tsp ground turmeric	Salt and pepper

1. Cut the chicken into about 2½ cm (1 inch) cubes and lightly season with salt and pepper.
2. In a large bowl, mix the curry paste, chutney, turmeric, oil and vinegar.
3. Toss in the chicken and turn to coat in the marinade - score the surface of the chicken pieces with the tip of a sharp kitchen knife a few timcs to allow the meat absorb the flavour. Cover and store in a cool place for 2 - 3 hours or overnight in the fridge.
4. Turn on your grill to maximum.
5. Place the chicken pieces in a single layer in a shallow oven tray and spoon over any remaining marinade. Cook under the hot grill for 6 - 8 minutes on each side or until cooked all the way through. Keep an eye on the chicken as it could easily burn. Remove from the oven.
6. Let it cool in the sauce until ready to serve.

The grilled chicken will keep in the fridge for up to 1 day.

To heat:

Either briefly warm in a microwave for 1 - 2 minutes. Or follow the same instructions as for the Persian chicken kebab (see page 87).

Chilli Duck Breast Wraps

These mini wraps are perfect for entertaining, easy to make and can be prepared in advance. The chilli duck breasts make a lovely platter for a buffet party and delightful main course or starter - see recipe on page 122.

Makes 16 - 18

    2 duck breasts, about 450 g (1 lb)
    Salt

For the marinade:

    ½ fresh red chilli, deseeded and finely
        chopped
    2 fat garlic clove, peeled and crushed
    2½ cm (1 in) piece of fresh ginger,
        peeled and grated (about 1 tsp)

    1½ tbsp clear honey
    Grated zest of 1 lemon
    Juice of ½ a lemon

For the wrap:

    9 pancakes from a pack (see Note
        following)
    About 200 ml 7 fl oz) plum sauce, such
        as Sherwood

    ½ cucumber, deseeded and finely sliced
        into 3 - 4 cm thin strips.
    5 spring onions trimmed and finely
        sliced into 3 - 4 cm thin strips
    2 - 3 tbsp chopped fresh coriander

1. Prick the duck skin all over with a fork and rub a little salt into the skin.
2. Mix all the ingredients for the marinade in an oven-proof dish.
3. Then toss in the duck breasts and turn to coat in the marinade. Cover and store in a cool place for a couple of hours or overnight in the fridge to allow the meat to absorb the flavour.
4. Pre-heat the oven to 200 °C / 400 °F / Gas mark 6.
5. Place the duck breasts in an small oven proof dish, skin side up, and roast for 30 - 35 minutes or until the skin is golden brown and the flesh tender. Remove from the oven and allow to cool.
6. Discard the skins. Thinly slice the meat and toss in the juices left from the cooking.
7. Cut each pancake in half, making sure to cover the remaining pancakes with foil while you work so that they do not dry out.

8. Spread 1 teaspoonful of plum sauce across each half of the pancake, then top with a couple of slices of duck, spring onions, cucumber and a sprinkle of coriander. Carefully roll up the pancake and place in an oven-proof dish. Tightly cover the dish with cling film so that the pancakes won't dry out. Keep in a cool place for not more than 40 minutes but do not refrigerate.

9. When ready to serve, remove the cover and warm the wraps through in a hot oven (200 °C / 400 °F / Gas mark 6) for about 2 minutes or in a microwave for 20 - 25 seconds. Keep a close eye on them, as the wraps dry out quickly.

Note:

Packs of ready-made pancakes for Peking duck are available in most oriental supermarkets and Chinese restaurants.

Prepare ahead:

Duck prepared to the end of step 6 keeps well in the fridge for up to 1 day.

To use:

A couple of hours before serving, place a non-stick frying pan over a high heat. Once it is very hot, place the duck slices in the dry pan and very briefly heat through for 20 - 30 seconds on each side. Then continue from step 7.

Oven Baked Honey & Chilli Sausages

These delicious sausages can be cooked 2 - 3 hours in advance and served at room temperature.
Makes 60

60 cocktail sausages	4 tbsp chilli sauce
4 tbsp runny honey	2 tbsp sesame seeds

1. Pre-heat the oven to 200 °C / 400 °F / Gas mark 6.
2. Grease a roasting tin. Add the sausages and cook for 20 minutes - see Note below. Remove the tin from the oven and drain off the fat.
3. Mix the honey, chilli sauce and sesame seeds and pour over the sausages. Carefully toss to coat. Cook for a further 20 - 30 minutes or until the sausages are golden. Serve with cocktail sticks to spear.

Note:

Every 10 minutes, give the tin a shake. It prevents the sausages from sticking to the tin, and helps the sausages to brown all over.

Oven Baked Sausages with Sherry, Soy Sauce & Honey

Replace the honey, chilli sauce and sesame seeds with a dressing of:
> 1 tbsp of soy sauce
>
> 1 tbsp each of sherry, runny honey and sesame oil

1. In a small bowl, mix all the ingredients for the dressing
2. Place the sausages in a greased roasting tin. Then pour over the dressing. Carefully toss to coat.
3. Cook the sausages in a pre-heated oven (200 °C / 400 °F / Gas mark 6) for 40 - 50 minutes or until they are golden.

See note under the Oven Baked Honey and Chilli Sausages recipe.

Prepare ahead:

The baked sausages will keep in the fridge for up to 2 days.

To use:

Either reheat in a hot oven (200 °C / 400 °F / Gas mark 6) for 3 - 5 minutes or briefly warm in a microwave for 1 - 2 minutes.

Horseradish Beef Fillet on Mini Yorkshire Puddings

These elegant bites are easy to prepare. The roast beef, Yorkshire puddings and sauce will keep in the fridge for up to 2 days. To assemble, before serving see tip below. A platter of this finely sliced beef fillet accompanied by a bowl of horseradish sauce can also enhance your buffet table. This Horseradish Beef fillet served with light mini Yorkshire puddings and a plate of roasted vegetables also makes an elegant main course.

Makes about 35 canapés

For the horseradish sauce:

1 x 140 ml carton double cream	3 - 3½ tbsp jarred horseradish sauce

For the Yorkshire puddings:

125 g (5 oz) plain white flour, sifted	2 tbsp vegetable oil
300 ml (½ pint) milk	Salt and pepper
1 medium egg, lightly beaten	Vegetable oil for oiling
½ tsp English mustard	

For the beef:

1 tbsp soft brown sugar	About 400 g (14 oz) (beef fillet
1 tsp English mustard	Salt and pepper
25 g (1 oz) softened butter	

To garnish:

Watercress leaves

1. Use non-stick mini muffin tins.
2. First make the sauce. Whisk the cream until thick. Add the horseradish and season to taste with salt and pepper. Cover and chill.
3. In a large bowl, place all the ingredients for the Yorkshire puddings and whisk together until smooth. Season with salt and pepper, then pour the batter into a jug and set aside.
4. Pre-heat the oven to 220 °C / 425 °F / Gas mark 7.
5. Mix the sugar, mustard and butter in a small bowl and then rub the mixture over the beef. Place the meat in a small roasting tin and cook for about 20 minutes for rare and 30 minutes for medium, turning over half way during cooking. Remove the beef from the oven and let it rest for 15 - 20 minutes.
6. Drizzle about 1 - 1½ teaspoon of oil (depending on the size of the tin) in each mini muffin tin. Then place them in the oven for 3 - 4 minutes until the oil is sizzling hot. Remove from the oven and quickly fill cups about 2/3 full with the batter, then immediately return them to the oven and cook for 10 - 12 minutes or until risen and golden. Remove the puddings from the tins and place on a wire rack.
7. Thinly slice the beef.
8. To serve, place a slice of beef on each warm pudding then top with a teaspoonful of horseradish sauce and a piece of watercress.

Prepare ahead:

For the beef: Slice the cooked beef and stack the slices on top of each other to avoid discolouration. Cover tightly with cling film. It keeps well in the fridge for up to 2 days.

To use:

Place a non-stick frying pan over a high heat. Once it is very hot, place the beef slices in the dry pan and very briefly heat through for 15 - 20 seconds on each side.

For the Yorkshire puddings:

Cold Yorkshire puddings keep well in an airtight tin for up to 2 days. When ready to use, warm them through in a pre-heated oven (180 °C / 350 °F / Gas mark 4) for 1 - 2 minutes.

To freeze:

Place the cold puddings in a single layer in a large container. Lay a piece of waxed paper on top of the puddings and repeat the process until all puddings have been used. Cover the top with another piece of waxed paper. Tightly secure the lid of the container, then wrap fully in a freezer bag and freeze. Remember to put a date on the container. They keep well in the freezer for up to 1 month.

To use:

Thaw the puddings overnight in the fridge or leave out in your kitchen to defrost for about 2 - 3 hours. Reheat in a pre-heated oven (180 °C / 350 °F / Gas mark 4) for 1 - 2 minutes. Then assemble the canapés.

Horseradish Beef Fillet on Oven-roasted Baby Potatoes

You may replace the Yorkshire puddings with roasted baby potato halves - see page 77. Prepare and cook the beef as instructed above.

To serve:
Place a slice of beef on each warm baby potato half then top with a teaspoonful of horseradish sauce and a piece of watercress.

Persian Style Meatballs with Coriander & Tomato Sauce

If possible, poach meatballs in the sauce 1 - 2 days in advance to allow the flavour to develop. Just reheat before serving.

The meatballs make a delicious main course - see recipe on page 125.

Makes about 25 - 30 meatballs
>   1 medium onion, peeled and roughly chopped
>   500 g (1 lb 2 oz) best quality lean minced beef
>   2 fat garlic cloves, peeled and crushed
>   1 large egg, beaten
>   1 tsp ground cumin
>   ½ tsp ground cinnamon
>   ½ tsp cayenne pepper or hot chilli powder
>   Salt
>   Oil for frying, about 1 - 2 tbsp

For the tomato sauce:
>   1 tbsp olive oil
>   2 fat garlic cloves, peeled and crushed
>   1 x 400 g tin of chopped tomato

>   3 tbsp water
>   Pinch of sugar
>   Salt and pepper

To garnish:
>   2 tbsp chopped fresh coriander.

1. Place the onion in a food processor and blend for a few seconds until it is roughly minced. Make sure the onion does not become too wet because this makes the meatballs soggy.

2. Then add the meat, garlic, egg, cumin, cinnamon, cayenne pepper and salt. Blend for a few seconds until the mixture becomes a paste.

3. Wet your hands then shape the mixture into 25 - 30 walnut-sized balls.

4. Heat the oil in a non-stick frying pan, add the meatballs and fry until evenly golden browned on the outside. Then transfer to a plate.

5. In the same pan, heat the 1 tbsp of oil; add the garlic, tomatoes, water and a pinch of sugar. Stir to combine, then transfer the sauce into a saucepan. Bring to a boil, cover and simmer over a low heat for about 5 minutes. Taste and adjust the seasoning.

6. Tip in the meatballs, stir gently, cover and cook for a further 15 - 20 minutes until the sauce coats the meatballs. Remove from the heat.

7. Place the meatballs in a serving dish and sprinkle with coriander.

8. Serve with a refreshing dip such as sour cream flavoured with chives or Persian style mint yoghurt (see page 71) and cocktail sticks to spear.

TIP:

- You can substitute beef with lamb, if you wish.

Prepare ahead:

The meatballs prepared to the end of step 4 will keep in the fridge for up to 2 days and in the freezer for up to 1 month. The tomato sauce prepared at step 5 will keep in the fridge for up to 1 week and in the freezer for up to 2 months.

Canapé Parties

Offer your guests a colourful, refreshing cocktail alongside a tray of attractive canapés to add a classy element to your party - see Delicious Drinks page 34.

The canapés in this section can be prepared 1 - 2 days in advance and some freeze well ahead of time. They can then be assembled on the day. Here are few suggestions.

MENU IDEAS

- Oven-baked honey and chilli sausages - see page 90
- Boursin cheese puffs with sesame and poppy seeds - see page 83
- Gently spiced prawns with mango chutney yoghurt dip - see page 85
- Smoked rainbow trout with chives on pumpernickel - see page 79

ᔣᕼᔤ

- Salmon, crème fraiche and horseradish with crostini - see page 78
- Gently spiced roast potato wedges served with sour cream flavoured with chives - see page 76
- Sweet piquante peppers stuffed with feta cheese, walnut or pecan nut - see page 80
- Persian meatballs with coriander and tomato sauce served with Persian style mint yoghurt - see pages 93, 71

ᔣᕼᔤ

- Roasted butternut squash and ginger soup "served in mini cups" - see page 99
- Mini tomatoes sandwiches with mozzarella and basil - see page 80
- Smoked rainbow trout with chives on pumpernickel - see page 79
- Persian style chicken kebab with a bowl of natural yoghurt - see page 87

ᔣᕼᔤ

- Chilled tomato, pepper and basil soup "served in mini cups" - see page 101
- Cucumber / Courgette with garlic and herb boursin - see page 81
- Curried parsnip chips served with sour cream - see page 75
- Horseradish beef fillet on mini Yorkshire puddings - see page 91

ᔣᕼᔤ

If you also want to offer some sweet nibbles, check the section for suggested ideas for Light Bites - see page 187

Roasted butternut squash and ginger soup

Scrumptious Soups

A bowl of soup makes a warming starter in the winter and a refreshing first course on a warm summer's day.

I love the delicate taste of puréed vegetable soups which is dominated mainly by the pure flavour of vegetables, making them a great starter to any meal. Serve soups in small portions to leave room for the main course and pudding.

All the soups in this section keep well in the fridge for up to 2 days. Reheat by simmering slowly, without allowing to boil.

Most vegetable soups freeze well. When you are ready to use, thaw the soup overnight in the fridge.

What I like about making soups is that you can turn simple ingredients into a delicious meal with a little time and effort, just by bearing in mind a few simple tips.

TIPS:

- Slice vegetables uniformly for even cooking, otherwise you will have underdone and overdone vegetables in your soup.

- Sauté onion, then add the vegetables, season, cover and cook over a low-medium heat for 5 - 6 minutes or until the vegetables starting to soften, stirring regularly. Next add the water and stir well. Cover the pan and simmer until the vegetables are tender and have given their flavour to the broth.

- It is easier to purée soup in small batches. Always cool the soup for a few minutes before pouring into a blender. Make sure the lid has an open vent hole to let the steam escape.

- You can make your soup more enticing either by stirring in a dollop of crème fraiche / natural Greek yoghurt, a sprinkle of chopped herbs or enliven it with a dash of lime juice or tobacco sauce. Test cautiously because less is more, so use sparingly as they can overpower the flavour of your soup and spoil it.

Aromatic Spinach & Coconut Soup

Subtle flavours of lemon grass and coconut fuse delicately in this simple soup.

Serves 5 - 6

Vegetarian

2 tbsp mild olive oil

2 bunches of spring onion, trimmed and finely chopped

1 red chilli, deseeded and finely chopped

2 garlic cloves, peeled and crushed

2½ cm (1 in) piece of fresh ginger, peeled and finely grated, about 1 - 1½ tsp, to taste

5 - 6 stalk lemon grass, outer skin removed and finely chopped

1 vegetable stock cube, softened in 3 tbsp water

900 ml (1½ pint) water

450 g (1 lb) fresh spinach, washed and roughly chopped

500 ml (18 fl oz) coconut milk

Squeeze of lemon juice (optional)   Salt and pepper

To garnish:
A small handful of chopped fresh parsley

1. Heat the oil in a large saucepan. Add the spring onions, chilli, garlic, ginger and lemon grass and cook over a low heat for about 5 minutes, stirring often, until spring onions lightly golden brown.
2. Stir in the vegetable stock and water. Bring to the boil, cover and simmer over a low heat for 10 - 12 minutes. Then add the spinach and coconut milk and simmer for a further 2 - 3 minutes or until the spinach is just cooked.
3. Cool the soup slightly. Transfer into a liquidiser and blend until smooth. Taste and adjust the seasoning.
4. Ladle into warm bowls and garnish before taking to the table.

Courgette & Gruyere Soup

This simple yet pleasant soup makes a lovely starter for a dinner party. The delicate shreds of Gruyere add a contrasting texture to the dish.

Serves 4

Vegetarian

3 tbsp olive oil

700 g (1½ lb) courgettes, trimmed and finely chopped

3 fat garlic cloves, peeled and finely chopped

1 vegetable or chicken stock cube, soften in 3 tbsp water

750 ml (1¼ pint) water

150 g (5 oz) grated Gruyere cheese, to taste

Salt and pepper

To garnish:
A small handful of chopped fresh parsley.

1. Heat the oil in a large saucepan over a medium heat. Add the courgettes, garlic and lightly season with salt and pepper. Stir well and then cover and cook for 5 - 6 minutes or until the courgettes are lightly browned and softened, stirring regularly.
2. Stir in the vegetable or chicken stock and water. Bring to the boil. Cover and simmer over a low heat for 10 - 12 minutes. Remove from the heat.
3. Cool the soup slightly. Transfer into a liquidiser and blend until smooth. Taste and adjust the seasoning.
4. When ready to serve, ladle the soup into warm bowls. Stir in a spoonful of grated Gruyere and scatter the parsley over the soup.

Courgette & Stilton Soup

Make the recipe in the same way. Just replace the Gruyere cheese with finely chopped Stilton.

Roasted Butternut Squash & Ginger Soup

A gentle hint of fresh ginger adds piquancy to this golden soup.

Serves 5 - 7

Vegetarian

1 medium butternut squash, about 700 g (1½ lb)

4 - 5 tbsp olive oil

1 medium onion, peeled and finely chopped

2 large carrots, peeled and finely chopped

300 g (11 oz) potatoes, peeled and diced

1 tsp turmeric

1 fat garlic clove, peeled and crushed

1 medium red chilli, deseeded and chopped or a pinch of dried chilli flakes

2½ cm (1 in) piece of fresh ginger, peeled and finely grated, to taste

1 vegetable stock cube, softened in 3 tbsp water

1.3 litres (2 pints 4 fl oz) water

Salt and pepper

To garnish:

100 ml (4 fl oz) crème fraiche and a handful of chopped fresh parsley or coriander

1. Pre-heat the oven to 200 °C / 400 °F / Gas mark 6.
2. Cut the butternut squash into wedges, roughly 10 x5 cm (4 x 2 in) thick, with the skins left on. Remove the seeds. Place in a large roasting tin. Drizzle with 2 - 3 tbsp of oil, lightly season with salt and pepper and toss to coat. Then spread out into a single layer and roast in the oven for about 25 minutes or until the squash is tender. Turn the squash over half way during the cooking so that both sides are caramelized.
3. Meanwhile, heat the remaining 2 tbsp of oil in a large saucepan on medium heat and sauté the onion until lightly golden. Then add the carrots and potatoes, along with the turmeric, garlic, chilli, and ginger. Lightly season with salt and pepper and toss to coat.
   Cover and cook over a low-medium heat for 5 - 6 minutes or until the vegetables start to soften, stirring regularly. Then add the vegetable stock and water. Bring to the boil, cover and simmer over a low heat for about 15 minutes.
4. Remove the roasted squash from the oven. Cool slightly then slip off the skins. The add the squash and the juices from the roasting tin to the vegetables in the saucepan. Cover and simmer over a low heat for another 10 minutes. Remove from the heat.
5. Cool the soup slightly. Next purée in a liquidiser until smooth. Season to taste.
6. Serve in warm bowls with a dollop of crème fraiche and fresh herb sprinkled on top.

Prepare ahead:

The soup prepared to the end of step 5, keeps well in the freezer for up to 1 month.

VARIATION

Roasted Butternut Squash, Ginger & Coconut Soup

For a more robust flavour, add 200 ml (7 fl oz) coconut milk to the soup in the last 2 - 3 minutes of cooking at step 4.

Chestnut Soup

This tasty, light, velvety soup is very easy to make.
Serves 4 - 5
Vegetarian

Knob of butter, about 25 g (1 oz)
6 celery sticks, finely chopped
450 g (1 lb) frozen and defrosted
  chestnuts or
2 x 200 g (2 x 8 oz) vacuum-packed
  whole cooked chestnuts
1 tsp dried thyme

1 vegetable stock cube, softened in 3
  tbsp water
750 ml (1¼ pint) water
150 ml (6 fl oz) single cream
Dash of lime juice
Salt and pepper

To garnish:

Fresh chopped parsley

1. Melt the butter in a saucepan and cook the celery over a medium heat for 5 - 6 minutes or until starting to soften, stirring regularly. Then add the chestnuts, thyme, vegetable stock and water. Lightly season with salt and pepper, bring to the boil, cover and simmer over a low heat for 15 - 20 minutes.
2. Cool the soup slightly. Transfer into a liquidiser and blend until smooth.
3. Add the cream and a dash of lime juice. Season to taste.
4. Ladle into warm bowls and garnish.

Prepare ahead:

The soup prepared to the end of step 2 keeps well in the freezer for up to 1 month.

VARIATIONS

Chestnut Soup with Seared Scallops

Adding seared scallops to this soup brings an extra elegant touch to any dinner party.
Make the recipe in the same way.

For the scallops:

8 medium scallops, rinsed and pat-dried with kitchen paper	Knob of butter, about 25 g (1 oz) Salt and pepper

1. Lightly season the scallops with salt and pepper.
2. Melt the butter in a large non-stick frying pan over a medium-high heat. Place the scallops in a single layer into the pan. Cook on one side for 1½ - 2 minutes or until golden, gently pressing down with a spoon so they caramelise evenly. Turn over the scallops and cook the other side for the same length of time. Remove from the heat.
3. Ladle the soup into a wide plate. Place 2 scallops elegantly on top and garnish with the chopped parsley.

Chestnut Soup with Crispy Bacon

Make the recipe in the same way.

1. Finely dice 4 - 5 slices of thin-cut rashers of bacon.
2. Heat 1 tbsp of olive oil in a frying pan.
3. Add the bacon to the pan and cook over a medium heat for 3 - 4 minutes or until crisp and golden, then lift and drain on a kitchen paper.
4. Scatter a few warm crispy bacon cubes over the top of each bowl of soup before taking to the table.

Note:

Chestnuts - Vacuum packed whole cooked chestnuts are available in most supermarkets.

Chilled Tomato, Pepper & Basil / Coriander Soup

Serves 6 - 8

This light summer soup, bursting with flavours, is best served in small bowls, cups or wine glasses, accompanied with a chunk of ciabatta or sourdough bread.

Vegetarian

8 medium plum tomatoes, roughly chopped	1 red chilli, deseeded and finely chopped
1 cucumber, halved, seeds scoped out and roughly chopped	400 ml (14 fl oz) tomato juice
1 red pepper, deseeded and finely chopped	2 garlic cloves, peeled and crushed
	3 - 4 tbsp olive oil
1 medium red onion, peeled and finely chopped	75 ml (3 fl oz) red wine vinegar, to taste
	Salt and pepper

To garnish:

Half a bunch of fresh basil, shredded.

1. In a large bowl, place all the ingredients together, lightly season with salt and pepper and leave to marinade for at least one hour to release flavours. Then blend in a liquidiser. Taste and adjust the seasoning.
2. Serve in pretty bowls, cups or wine glasses garnished with the fresh herb.

Note:
You may replace the basil with chopped fresh coriander.

Seafood with ginger saffron sauce

Fish

I love the versatility of fish because you can create something that is both light and luxurious at the same time. The recipes in this section are flavoursome, easy and fairly quick to make.

Fish is very delicate, so a little extra care makes a big difference to the success of your dish. Here are a few tips, including tips for specific fish.

TIPS:

- Be careful not to cook fish for too long because it can easily disintegrate.
- Cooked fish flakes easily, so care is needed when transferring to a dish.
- **Prawns** - do not overcook prawns as they will shrink and become tough.
- **Scallops** - do not put too many scallops in the pan at one time. If you wish to caramelise scallops, cook them in small batches.
- **Cooking Salmon** – the flesh should still be a little pink in the middle. Remember that overcooking salmon ruins the soft flesh and it can become tough and tasteless very quickly whereas you can always put the fillets back in the oven for couple of minutes if you think they need more time.
- **Fish casserole** - firm fish such as: haddock, halibut, coley, pollack, hake, sea bass or monk fish tail holds together much better on cooking.

Mediterranean Fish Casserole

This tangy tomato-based casserole with chunky pieces of moist white fish, with slivers of pepper and fennel makes an elegant tasty dinner party dish.

Serve with potato wedges and a carrot, apple and fresh mint coleslaw - see pages 76, 160.

Serves 4

700 g (1½ lb) skinless firm white fish such as: cod, haddock, halibut, coley, pollack or hake

Dash of lime juice
Salt and pepper

For the sauce:

2 tbsp olive oil
1 large red onion, peeled and finely sliced
150 g (6 oz) fennel, finely sliced
1 red pepper, cut into 2 - 3 cm chunks
2 large garlic cloves, peeled and crushed
½ tsp smoked paprika or 1 tsp hot chilli powder
1 tsp dried thyme or oregano

1 x 400 g tin of chopped tomatoes
2 tbsp tomato paste
Juice of ½ - 1 fresh lime
Pinch of sugar
10 - 12 black olives, halved
Salt and pepper
3 - 4 tbsp mayonnaise or Greek natural yoghurt

To garnish:

A small handful of freshly chopped chives or parsley

Use a shallow baking dish, about 28 x 28 cm (11 x 11 in) or 30 x 25 cm (12 x 10 in)

1. First make the sauce. Heat the oil in a non-stick frying pan. Add the onion and fennel. Stir, cover and cook over a medium heat for about 5 minutes, stirring occasionally, until they are softened. Then add the red pepper, garlic, smoked paprika or chilli powder, thyme or oregano and lightly season with salt and pepper. Cover and cook for another 2 - 3 minutes, stirring regularly. Next add the tomatoes, tomato paste and a pinch of sugar. Stir to combine, then cover and simmer over a low heat for 5 - 6 minutes. Taste and season.
2. Meanwhile cut the fish into about 5 cm (2 in) chunks and pat dry.
3. Pre-heat the oven to 190 °C / 380 °F / Gas mark 5.
4. Place the fish in the baking dish, season with a dash of lime juice and salt and pepper. Spoon the sauce over the fish and scatter with the olives. Cover and bake in the pre-heated oven for about 25 - 30 minutes, depending on the thickness of the fish. Remove from the oven.
5. Gently stir in the mayonnaise or Greek yoghurt, being careful not to break up the fish. Scatter the herb over the sauce.

Note:

You may prepare the dish to the end of step 4 a couple of hours in advance. When ready to serve, warm through in a pre-heated oven (200 °C / 400 °F / Gas mark 6) for about 5 - 7 minutes. Then stir in the mayonnaise or Greek yoghurt.

Prepare ahead:

The sauce prepared to the end of step 1 will keep in the fridge for up to 2 days and freeze well for up to 1 month.

TIP:

- Replace the smoked paprika / hot chilli powder with a pinch of ground saffron and cayenne pepper.

Rosemary Prawns & Parma Ham Skewers

These light appetizing prawns are great for any formal or informal entertaining. They are just as easy to make for twenty people as they are for two.

Serve with baby potatoes with fresh chopped dill and buttermilk dressing and a beetroot salsa - see pages 158, 159.

The recipe for this dish is the same as the rosemary prawns and Parma ham skewers in the chapter on Easy and Elegant Dips, Canapés and Light Bites - see page 86.

It makes 8 skewers and serves 4.

You need 8 metal skewers or 8 wooden satay sticks, soaked in cold water for 30 - 40 minutes to prevent burning during cooking.

Make the recipe the same way - see page 86.

At step 2, after the each prawn has been wrapped in half a piece of Parma ham, thread 3 prawns onto a skewer or satay stick. Then continue from step 4.

Cajun Seafood Casserole

This tasty simple seafood with a touch of Cajun spices is easy to prepare and demands very little of your time.

Serve with a big bowl of crispy green salad

Serves 4 - 6

200 g (4 oz) uncooked long grain rice

250 ml (9 fl oz) dry white wine

20 - 25 raw fresh or frozen and
   defrosted peeled prawns

25 g (1 oz) butter

2 tbsp mild olive oil

700 g (1½ lb) skinless firm white fish
   such as cod, haddock, halibut, pollack
   or hake

Bunch of spring onions, trimmed and
   roughly hopped

1 large garlic clove, peeled and crushed

1 tsp paprika

1 tsp dried thyme

Dash of cayenne pepper

1 tbsp sun dried tomato paste

1 - 1½ tsp Dijon mustard

1 x 375 ml tub of single cream

Dash of lime juice (optional)

Salt and pepper

To garnish:

A handful of shredded basil leaves

Use a shallow baking dish, about 28 x 28 cm (11 x 11 in) or 30 x 25 cm (12 x 10 in).

1. Cook the rice following the instructions on the packet.
2. Cut the fish into about 5 cm (2 in) chunks pat dry and lightly season with salt and pepper.
3. Pour the wine into a medium saucepan and bring to a boil. Then toss in the prawns and simmer over a low heat for 1 - 2 minutes or until they turn a nice light red colour - see page 104. Remove the prawns from the pan with a slotted spoon and place in a bowl. Set aside the remaining wine.
4. Heat the oven to 200 °C / 400 °F / Gas mark 6.
5. Melt the butter with the 1 tbsp of oil in a large non-stick saucepan on a medium-high heat. Add the fish 3 - 4 pieces at a time and cook for 2 - 3 minutes on each side. Then remove to a plate.
6. Add the remaining 1 tbsp of oil to the same pan. Toss in the spring onions, stir and cook for 2 - 3 minutes or until it starts to soften.

7. Next add the herbs, spices, sun dried tomato paste, cream and the wine left over from the poached prawns. Bring to a boil. Then gently add the prawns and fish. Pop a lid on and cook over a low heat for 3 - 4 minutes. Be careful not to cook the fish for too long as it can disintegrate. Check the seasoning. Add a dash of lime juice if preferred.

8. Place the cooked rice in the oven-proof dish, arrange the fish over the rice, then pour over the sauce. Bake uncovered for about 10 - 12 minutes. Remove from the oven.

9. Garnish before taking to the table.

Prepare ahead:

You may use either of these TWO options:

1. Prepare the dish up to the end of step 7 a couple of hours in advance. A little while before serving, turn the oven on and carry out step 8.

2. Complete to the end of step 7 one day in advance. Cool the fish and rice, cover and refrigerate.

To use:

Warm up the rice, gently reheat the fish with the sauce and then carry out step 8.

Salmon Fillet Dishes

The glory of salmon is its versatility and quickness to cook. You may replace the salmon with trout fillet. Here I share with you four of my favourite recipes.

These salmon dishes are also delicious if served cold.

Oven Baked Salmon Fillet with Saffron & Citrus Dressing

In this dish, the salmon is delicately flavoured with a tangy dressing of fresh orange and lime juice, infused with a hint of saffron and ginger.

Serve with fragrant turmeric and cinnamon rice or Persian style couscous (see pages 133, 135) and a lightly cooked mix of green beans and sugar snap peas.

Serves 4

200 ml (7 fl oz) fresh orange juice
Juice of 1 fresh lime
1 tsp saffron threads, crushed
Or ¼ ground saffron
2½ cm (1 in) piece of fresh ginger
    Peeled and grated, about ½ tsp

1½ tbsp olive oil
4 x 150 g (6 oz) skinless salmon fillet
    lightly seasoned with salt and pepper
Salt and pepper

1. Pre-heat the oven to 200 °C / 400 °F / Gas mark 6.

2. Mix the orange and lime juice in a small saucepan and simmer over a high heat until the juice is reduced to about 100 ml (4 fl oz). Stir in the saffron, ginger and olive oil. Remove from the heat.

3. Place the salmon or trout fillets in a single layer on a baking dish. Pour the dressing over the fish. Roll the salmon in the dressing to fully absorb the flavours.
4. Bake uncovered in the oven for about 15 - 20 minutes (less if the fillet is thin) or until the fish is just cooked (see page 104). Remove the fish from the oven.
5. Transfer to a serving plate and spoon over the sauce.

Oven Baked Salmon with Warm Honey, Dill & Fresh Lime Dressing

In this recipe, replace the citrus dressing with:

Juice of 1 fresh lime

1½ tbsp olive oil

1 tsp Dijon mustard

1½ tsp honey

About 1 tsp dried dill or 1 - 1½ tbsp fresh chopped dill, to taste

Salt and pepper

In a small bowl, mix together all the ingredients for the dressing and lightly season with salt and pepper. Then follow from step 3.
Serve the salmon with boiled new potatoes and Waldorf salad - see page 159.

Oven Baked Salmon with Smoked Paprika, Coriander & Lime Juice

In this recipe, replace the citrus dressing with:

2 tbsp olive oil

Juice of 1 fresh lime

½ tsp smoked paprika, to taste

1 tbsp chopped fresh coriander

Pinch of salt

In a small bowl, mix together all the ingredients for the marinade. Then follow from step 3.
Serve the salmon with roasted sweet potato wedges and Persian style mint yoghurt -
see pages 150, 71.

Prepare ahead:
The salmon prepared to the end of step 4 keeps well in the fridge for up to 1 day.

To use:
If you want to serve the fish warm, bring it to room temperature. Then heat through in a hot oven (200 °C / 400 °F / Gas mark 6) for 2 - 3 minutes, turning the fish over half way through. Or briefly warm in a microwave for 1 - 2 minutes.

Roasted Salmon Teriyaki with Salsa of Sweet Chilli & Mint

This simple dish is delightfully delicious. It can be served either hot or at room temperature. Serve with a crispy green salad and Persian Style Couscous with toasted pine nuts - see page 135.
Serves 4

2 tbsp olive oil

300 g (11 oz) carrots, peeled and cut into 2½ cm (1 in) thin strips

1 large red pepper, deseeded and cut into thin strips

1 bunch of spring onions, trimmed and
    cut into thin strips
2 large garlic cloves, peeled and crushed
2½ cm (1 in) piece of fresh ginger,
    peeled and grated, about 1 - 1½ tsp

3 tbsp teriyaki sauce
4 x 150 g (6 oz) skinless salmon fillet or
    trout, lightly seasoned with salt and
    pepper
Salt

For the sweet chilli and mint salsa:

3 tbsp rice vinegar or white wine vinegar
2 tbsp caster sugar
¼ cucumber, finely chopped
1 small red chilli, deseeded and finely
    chopped

2 tbsp chopped fresh mint or ½ tsp
    dried mint
2½ cm (1 in) piece of fresh ginger,
    peeled and grated
Salt

1. Heat the oil in a large saucepan. Add the vegetables, garlic and ginger. Lightly season with salt, cover and cook on a medium heat for 3 - 4 minutes, stirring regularly until the vegetables are just soft. Then stir in teriyaki sauce and mix well. Remove from the heat and set aside to cool.
2. Pre-heat the oven to 200 °C / 400 °F / Gas mark 6.
3. Place the fish fillets in a single layer on a baking dish. Spoon an equal amount of the vegetables on top of each salmon or trout, and then cover the dish with foil.
4. Place in the oven and cook for 20 - 25 minutes or until the fish is just cooked. Place a skewer in the centre of the fish. If it feels cool, cook for another 4 - 6 minutes. Remove from the oven and let it rest for 5 minutes.
5. Meanwhile make the salsa. In a medium bowl, whisk together the vinegar and sugar then add the rest of the salsa ingredients. Season to taste with salt.
6. Carefully transfer the fish to a serving plate and spoon over some of the salsa.

Note:

For a buffet party, you may replace the individual salmon fillets with a whole fillet, 600 g (1 lb 5 oz).

Make the recipe in the same way but at step 4 cook the fish for 25 - 35 minutes or until it is cooked through. Place a skewer in the centre of the fish. If it feels cool, cook for another 5 - 10 minutes.

Prepare ahead:

The salsa without mint keeps well in the fridge for up to 2 days. Just add the fresh mint before serving. The fish prepared to the end of step 3 keeps well in the fridge up to 1 day.

To use:

Bring the fish to the room temperature before placing it in the oven.

Seafood Rendezvous with Ginger, Coriander, Lime, Coconut & Chilli

This light and pleasant dish is also delicious if served at room temperature. Serve with Fragrant Turmeric & Cinnamon Rice and beetroot salsa - see pages 133, 159.

Serves 5 - 6

600 g (1 lb 5 oz) mixed skinless white fish such as: cod, halibut, monk fish, pollack or hake

450 g (1 lb) large raw fresh or frozen and defrosted peeled prawns

3 tbsp sunflower or rapeseed oil

2 small red onions, peeled and finely chopped

3 garlic cloves, finely chopped

1 red chilli deseeded and finely chopped

2½ cm (1 in) piece of fresh ginger, peeled and grated, about 1 - 1½ tsp, to taste

300 ml (7 fl oz) light coconut milk

1 fish stock cube, soften in 2 tbsp water

Grated zest of 1 lime

Juice of 1½ - 2 fresh limes

Salt and pepper

To garnish:

A handful of freshly chopped coriander, about 75 g (3 oz), plus extra for garnish

1. Cut the fish into about 5 cm (2 in) chunks and lightly season with salt and pepper.
2. Pat dry the prawns.
3. Heat 1 tbsp of oil in a large non–stick saucepan over a medium heat. Toss in the prawns and cook for 1 - 2 minutes or until they turn a nice light red colour - see page 104. Remove the prawns from the pan with a slotted spoon and place in a bowl.
4. Add the remaining 2 tbsp of oil to the same pan. When the oil is fairly hot add the fish and cook on a medium heat for about 2 minutes on each side. Remove the fish with a slotted spoon and transfer to a plate.
5. Add the onions to the same pan, drizzling with a little more oil if too dry and sauté over a medium-low heat for 3 - 4 minutes or until they are softened - scraping up any bits of fish stuck to the pan. Then add the garlic, chilli and ginger and cook for 30 - 40 seconds before stirring in the coconut milk, fish stock, lime zest and lime juice. Bring to a boil, cover and simmer over a low heat for 4 - 5 minutes.
6. Next add the prawns, fish and coriander. Carefully move them around in the sauce, keeping pieces intact. Put the lid back and simmer over a low heat for about 4 - 5 minutes or until the fish is just cooked. Be careful not to cook the fish for too long as it can easily disintegrate. Taste and adjust the seasoning. Remove from the heat.
7. Sprinkle the coriander over the seafood before taking to the table.

Note:

You may prepare the dish to the end of step 6, couple of hours in advance. When ready to serve, gently warm through over a medium-low heat for about 2 - 4 minutes.

Prepare ahead:

Complete to the end of step 5, one day in advance, chill, cover and refrigerate.

To use:

Bring the prawns and fish to room temperature and gently reheat the sauce before carrying out step 6.

Lime Chilli Prawns with Avocado Salsa

This simple flavourful dish looks very attractive. It is good accompanied with a warm fluffy Persian style couscous and crunchy coleslaw with light orange dressing - see pages 135, 162.

Serves 4

200 g (7 oz) cooked fresh or frozen and defrosted peeled king prawns

2 tbsp sunflower or rapeseed oil

2 garlic cloves, peeled and crushed

1 red chilli, deseeded and finely chopped

Juice of 1 fresh lime

1 small red onion, peeled and finely chopped

300 g (11 oz) cherry tomatoes cut in half

4 spring onions trimmed and finely chopped

1 - 2 tbsp freshly chopped coriander

2 large ripe avocadoes

1 - 2 tbsp olive oil

Dash of lime juice

Salt and pepper

1. Pat dry the prawns with a with kitchen paper.
2. In a non-stick frying pan, heat the oil over a medium-high heat. Add the prawns, garlic, chilli and lime juice. Lightly season with salt. Toss to coat and cook for 2 - 3 minutes, stirring regularly so that the prawns can absorb the flavours - see page 104. Remove the prawns from the pan with a slotted spoon and place in a bowl. Leave the remaining sauce in the pan.
3. Then simmer the sauce in the pan over a high heat for 2 - 3 minutes or until the mixture is fairly thick. Remove from the heat.
4. Next pour the sauce over the prawns. Stir to combine, cool and cover. Store the prawns in a fridge for 2 - 3 hours or overnight, allowing them to absorb maximum flavour.
5. In a large bowl, mix the prawns and its sauce with the red onion, tomatoes, spring onion and coriander.
6. Stone, peel and dice the avocadoes. Drizzle with the olive oil and lime juice to delay browning. Toss gently.
7. Add the avocado chunks to the prawn mixture and carefully mix. Taste and adjust the seasoning.
8. Push the avocado stones into the salad and cover tightly with cling film.
9. When ready to serve, remove the avocado stones from the salad.

Prepare ahead:

The dish prepared to the end of step 5 keeps well in the fridge for up to 1 day. Add the avocadoes to the prawns 3 - 4 hours before serving. Push the avocado stones into the salad and cover tightly with cling film and refrigerate.

Seafood with Ginger Saffron Sauce

This dish with its pale golden colour and slightly tart sauce is easy and quick to make. It is also delicious if served at room temperature.

Serve with boiled new potatoes, al dente sugar snap peas, and a platter of grilled vegetables - see page 147.

Serves 4 - 5

4 x 150 g (6 oz) skinless salmon fillet or trout cut into 5 cm (2 in) chunks

300 ml (12 fl oz) dry white wine

16 - 20 raw fresh or frozen and defrosted peeled prawns

2 tbsp olive oil

8 - 12 medium scallops, rinsed and pat dried with kitchen paper

1 small leek and carrot each about 75 g (30 oz) washed, trimmed and finely chopped

1 fish stock cube, soften in 100 ml hot water

2½ cm (1 in) piece of fresh ginger, peeled and grated - about 1 tsp to taste

1 tsp saffron threads, crushed or a pinch of ground saffron

2 - 3 tbsp crème fraiche

Dash of lime juice

Salt and pepper

To garnish:

A small handful of shredded basil leaves

1. Pre-heat the oven to 200 °C / 400 °F / Gas mark 6.
2. Lay the salmon or trout pieces in a single layer in a shallow baking dish, lightly season with salt and pepper and drizzle with 50 ml (2 fl oz) of white wine. Bake uncovered in the oven for about 8 minutes (less if the fillet is thin) or until the fish is just cooked.
3. Meanwhile pour the remaining 250 ml (10 fl oz) wine into a saucepan. Bring to a boil then toss in the prawns and simmer over a low heat for 1 - 2 minutes, until they turn a nice light red colour. Remove the prawns from the pan with a slotted spoon and place in a bowl. Set aside the remaining wine.
4. Place a large non-stick saucepan on a medium-high heat, add 1 tbsp of olive oil and swirl it around the pan. When the oil is hot, place the scallops in a single layer into the pan. Season them lightly with salt and pepper and cook on one side for 1½ - 2 minutes or until golden, gently pressing down with a spoon so they caramelise evenly. Turn over the scallops and cook the other side for the same length of time. Remove to a plate.
5. Add the remaining 1 tbsp of oil to the same pan and sauté the leek over a medium heat for 1 - 2 minutes. Next add the carrot, lightly season with salt and pepper and mix well. Cover and sweat the vegetables over a low heat for 4 - 5 minutes or until softened.
6. Then stir in the fish stock, ginger, saffron and the wine which is left over from poaching the prawns. Bring to a boil, pop a lid on and simmer over a low heat for about 5 minutes.
7. Remove the lid and stir in the crème fraiche. The sauce should have the consistency of a thin cream. Add the prawns, scallops and salmon with its juices from the pan. Gently stir

to coat, being careful not to break up the fish. Cover and simmer over a low heat for 3 - 4 minutes - see page 104.

8. Check the seasoning. Add a dash of lime juice if preferred.
9. Garnish before taking to the table.

Note:

You may prepare the dish to the end of step 7, couple of hours in advance. Remove from the heat. When ready to serve, gently warm through over a medium-low heat for about 2 - 4 minutes. Then carry out step 8

Prepare ahead:

Complete to the end of step 6 one day in advance, chill, cover and refrigerate.

To use:

Bring the fish to room temperature and gently reheat the sauce before carrying out step 7.

TIP:

- You may replace the salmon with sea bass or monk fish tail.

Scallops and tomatoes

Pan Seared Scallops with Oven Roasted Tomatoes

The flavour of the roasted tomatoes goes very well with the sweet dense flesh of the scallops. This tasty dish made with just a few ingredients makes a quick, light and luxurious starter or a main course for a small group.

Serve with roasted sweet potatoes wedges - see page 150 and steamed asparagus.

Serves 4 as main course. See Tip below if you would like to serve as a starter.

16 large or 20 medium sized scallops cleaned	4 tbsp olive oil
	20 cherry tomatoes, cut in half
2 garlic cloves, peeled and crushed	Juice of 1 lime
1½ tsp dried thyme	Salt and pepper

To garnish:

Shredded basil leaves

TIP:

- As a starter, you may serve 2 - 3 large or 3 - 4 medium scallops per head with a small handful of crispy salad leaves.

---

1. Pre-heat the oven to 200 °C / 400 °F / Gas mark 6.
2. Rinse the scallops and pat dry with kitchen paper.
3. In a large bowl, mix the garlic, thyme and 2 tbsp of olive oil. Then toss in the scallops, lightly season with salt and pepper and gently turn to coat with the dressing. Set aside.
4. Place the tomatoes in one layer in a shallow roasting tin skin side down. Season with salt and pepper. Drizzle with the remaining 2 tbsp of oil and roast in the oven for about 10 minutes or until tender but still holding shape.
5. Meanwhile place a large non-stick frying pan over a high heat. When it is hot, reduce the heat to a medium-high and place the scallops in a single layer into the pan. Cook on one side for 1½ - 2 minutes or until golden, gently pressing down with a spoon so that they caramelise evenly. Turn over the scallops and cook the other side for the same length of time. Then drizzle with the lime juice.
6. Carefully add the tomatoes and their juice to the scallops and gently mix. Remove from the heat.
7. Garnish before taking to the table.

Prepare ahead:

2 - 3 hours in advance, roast the tomatoes and sear the scallops and transfer them with their juices into a bowl. Set aside the frying pan for later use.

To use:

Heat the same frying pan over a low heat, add 1 tbsp of hot water and stir to scrape away any sticky brown sediment from the pan. Then gently add the scallops and tomatoes. Carefully stir and reheat for 1 - 2 minutes.

It is impossible to write a book on entertaining and cooking without including chicken and duck recipes because they are so popular and, again, versatile.

Chicken with Orange, Cardamom & Pan Roasted Pepper

The combination of fresh orange juice, orange marmalade and cardamom gives a gentle sweet fragrant flavour to this Persian dish. It tastes even better if prepared one day in advance.
Serve with fragrant turmeric and cinnamon rice (see page 133) and a bowl of crispy green salad.
Serves 7 - 8

900 g (2 lbs) chicken breast fillets or chicken thighs (already boned and skinned)

4 - 5 tbsp olive oil

2 tsp ground turmeric

7 - 8 cardamom pods, lightly crushed and husk removed - see page 66

2 medium red onions, peeled and finely sliced

3 red and 2 green peppers, deseeded and cut into about 2½ cm (1 in) chunks

2 tbsp levelled flour

600 ml (1 pint) good quality orange juice

2 - 3 tbsp orange marmalade

2 - 2½ tsp Dijon mustard

1 chicken stock cube, softened in 2 tbsp water

Salt and pepper

To garnish:
A small handful of chopped pistachio or fresh mint leaves

1. Cut the chicken into about 2½ cm (1 in) bite-size pieces and season with salt and pepper.
2. In a large saucepan, heat 2 tbsp of oil on a high-medium heat and brown the chicken a few pieces at a time for 2 - 3 minutes on each side, adding a little more oil if necessary. Sprinkle with turmeric and cardamom and mix well and cook for another 30 - 40 seconds until the chicken pieces are coated with the spices. Then transfer them to a plate.
3. In the same pan, heat the remaining 2 - 3 tbsp of oil and sauté the onions over a medium heat, until lightly golden. Then add the peppers, lightly season with salt and pepper, cover and cook for 3 - 4 minutes, stirring regularly.
4. Add the browned chicken and flour to the pan. Mix well before stirring in the orange juice, orange marmalade, mustard and chicken stock. Stir to combine, then bring to the boil. Cover and simmer over a low heat for 15 - 20 minutes or until the chicken is cooked all the way through and peppers are soft. Season to taste.
5. Transfer to a deep serving dish.
6. Garnish before taking to the table.

Note:
You may prepare the dish to the end of step 4 a couple of hours in advance. When ready to serve, gently warm through over a medium-low heat for about 2 - 4 minutes. Then carry out step 5.

Prepare ahead:

The chicken and the sautéed onions and peppers prepared to the end of 3 keep well in the fridge for up to 2 days and in the freezer for up to 1 month.

Pan Roasted Chicken with Prunes & Ginger

In this typical Persian winter dish, the spices are fried with the chicken to sear the flavour into the meat.

Serve with saffron couscous and carrot, apple and mint coleslaw - see pages 136, 160.

Serves 4 - 6

600 g (1 lb 5 oz) chicken breast fillets

3 - 4 tbsp mild olive oil

1 tsp ground turmeric

1 tsp ground cinnamon

2 garlic cloves, peeled and crushed

2½ cm (1 in) piece of fresh ginger, peeled and grated, about 2 - 2½ tsp, to taste

1 medium onion, peeled and finely sliced

1 small potato, about 200 g (7 oz) such as King Edwards, peeled and cut into 2½ cm (1 in) chunks

300 g (11 oz) ready to eat stoned prunes

1 chicken stock cube, softened in 2 tbsp water

600 ml (1 pint) warm water

2 tsp sugar

3 tbsp fresh lemon juice

Salt and pepper

To garnish:

A small handful of fresh chopped parsley

1. Cut the chicken into about 2½ cm (1 in) bite-size pieces and season with salt and pepper.
2. Heat 1 tbsp of oil in a large non-stick saucepan on a high-medium heat and brown the chicken a few pieces at a time for 2 - 3 minutes on each side, adding a little more oil if necessary. Next sprinkle over the turmeric, cinnamon, garlic and ginger. Stir well and cook for another 35 - 40 seconds until the chicken pieces are coated with the spices. Then transfer them to a plate.
3. In the same pan, heat the remaining 2 - 3 tbsp of oil and sauté the onion over a medium heat until lightly golden.
4. Add the potato, lightly season with salt and pepper and cook for 3 - 4 minutes until lightly coloured.
5. Next, tip in the chicken, prunes, chicken stock, water, sugar and lemon juice. Stir to combine, then bring to the boil. Cover and simmer over a low heat for about 20 minutes or until the chicken is cooked all the way through and potatoes are soft. Remove from the heat.
6. Use a fork to press the prunes so as to break them up. This is important to give a dark chocolate colour to the sauce. Taste and adjust the seasoning.
7. Transfer to a deep serving dish. Carefully arrange the chicken and potatoes then spoon over the sauce.
8. Garnish before taking to the table.

Note:

You may prepare the dish to the end of step 6, couple of hours in advance. When ready to serve, gently warm through over a medium – low heat for about 2 - 4 minutes. Then carry out step 7.

Prepare ahead:

You may use either of these TWO options:

1. Prepare the dish to the end of step 4. Chill, cover and refrigerate for up to 1 day. Bring to room temperature before carrying out step 5.
2. Prepare the chicken to the end of step 2. Chill cover and store in the freezer for up to 1 month. And the same goes for the sautéed onion prepared to the end of step 3. Thaw the chicken and sautéed onion overnight in the fridge before carrying out step 5.

Lightly Spiced Grilled Chicken with Fragrant Couscous

This colourful light dish is a centre-piece for a buffet. It also tastes good served at room temperature.

Serve with a salad of cannellini, beetroot and apple and a bowl of mixed crispy green salad (see page 143).

The recipe for the chicken in this dish is the same as the Lightly Spiced Grilled chicken Bites in Easy and Elegant Dips, Canapés and Light Bites, page 88.

Serves 8 - 10

For the chicken, make the recipe the same way as in the Lightly Spiced Grilled chicken Bites (see page 88) but just double the quantity.

For the fragrant couscous:

500 g (1 lb 2 oz) couscous	1 bunch of spring onion, trimmed and
4 tbsp mild olive oil	roughly chopped
1 tsp turmeric	Handful of fresh chopped mint
1 tsp cinnamon	Salt and pepper
300 g (11 oz) cherry tomatoes cut in half	

1. Cook the couscous following the instructions on the packet and then gently fluff it up with a fork.
2. Heat the oil in large sauce pan. Add the turmeric and cinnamon and cook over a medium heat for about 30 - 40 seconds before adding the couscous. Stir until all the grains are coated with spices.
3. Add the chicken with its juices to the couscous and season to taste.
4. Remove from the heat then gently stir in the spring onions, tomatoes and mint.

Note:

You may prepare the dish to the end of step 3, couple of hours in advance. When ready to serve, gently warm through over a medium –low heat for about 2 - 4 minutes. Then carry out step 4.

Prepare ahead:

This dish, prepared to the end of step 2, keeps well in the fridge for up to 1 day.

Smoked Chicken & Mango Salad

The sweetness of mango and sharpness of fresh lime juice works beautifully with smoked chicken.

Serve with a crispy green salad and quinoa with aduki beans salsa - see pages 136.

Serves 8 - 10

For the dressing:

3 - 4 tbsp sunflower or rapeseed oil

Juice of 1 - 2 limes, to taste

Grated zest of 2 limes

1 - 2 tbsp mayonnaise

For the salad:

1 smoked chicken, about 900 g (2 lbs)

1 cucumber, deseeded and sliced into thin strips about 2½ cm (1 in) long

1 large ripe mango, peeled, stone removed and flesh chopped into 2½ cm (1 in) cubes

1 bunch of spring onions, trimmed and finely chopped

1 small red onion, peeled and finely chopped

2 - 3 tbsp finely chopped fresh coriander

Salt and black pepper

1. In a small bowl, mix the oil, lime juice, lime zest, mayonnaise and any mango juice from your cutting board. Set aside.
2. Slice the chicken into about 2½ cm (1 in) bite-size pieces. Discard any skin and bone.
3. Place all the ingredients for the salad in a large bowl and pour over the dressing. Toss well. Taste and adjust the seasoning.

Prepare ahead:

This salad keeps well in the fridge for up to 1 day.

Note:

Smoked chicken is available in Waitrose and some other supermarkets.

Persian Style Chicken Salad with Chestnuts

Chestnut gives a subtle smokey flavour to this light salad. The dish takes no time to prepare and is ideal for a simple, stress-free buffet for any number of people.

Serve with saffron couscous and aduki beans salsa - see pages 136, 140.

Serves 6 - 8

700 g (1½ lb) cooked chicken breasts

200 g vacuum-packed whole cooked chestnuts

10 spring onions, trimmed and finely chopped

4 cos lettuces, finely chopped

1 Granny Smith apple unpeeled, cored and finely chopped

2 tbsp chopped fresh coriander or tarragon

200 ml (7 fl oz) light crème fraiche

284 ml (10 fl oz) buttermilk

salt and pepper

To garnish:

Salad cress

1. Slice the chicken into 2½ cm (1 in) bite-size pieces. Discard any skin.
2. In a large bowl, mix all the ingredients together. Season to taste and garnish.

Prepare ahead:

This salad keeps well in the fridge for up to 1 day.

Note:

Chestnuts - vacuum packed whole cooked chestnuts are available in most supermarkets.

Pan Roasted Duck Breast with Pomegranate & Walnut Sauce

In this simple yet elegant, classic Persian dish, the marriage of ground walnut and the sweet sour pomegranate juice add extra interest.

Serve with fluffy saffron rice (see page 132) and al dente sugar snap peas.

Serves 6

100 g (4 oz) walnut pieces

600 ml (1 pint) good quality pomegranate juice

2 tbsp mild olive oil

1 medium red onion, peeled and finely chopped

1 tsp turmeric

½ tsp cinnamon or mixed spice, to taste

1½ tbsp tomato paste

Dash of lime juice

6 duck breasts, about 200 g (7 oz) each

Salt and pepper

To garnish:

A handful of pomegranate seeds

Duck breast with saffron rice and sugar snap peas

1. Place the walnuts in a food processor and whizz to a purée.
2. Pour the pomegranate juice in a wide saucepan and simmer over a high heat for a few minutes until reduced to about 450 ml (16 fl oz), then set aside.

3. Heat 1 tbsp of oil in a large non-stick frying pan. Tip in the onion and sauté over a medium heat until soft and golden. Sprinkle over the turmeric and cinnamon and continue to cook 30 - 40 seconds. Add the ground walnuts and cook for another minute before adding the tomato paste and pomegranate juice. Stir to combine, then bring to the boil. Simmer uncovered over a medium heat for a few minutes, stirring occasionally, until the sauce has the consistency of thin cream. Add the lime juice and season with salt and pepper to taste. Transfer to a small saucepan and cover

4. Skin the duck breasts, retaining 2 pieces of skin for cooking. Season the meat with salt and pepper.

5. Heat 1 tbsp of oil in a large non-stick frying pan, add the duck skins and cook over a high heat until they turn crisp and golden brown, but not burning. Remove the skins, leaving the fat in the pan. You should now have about 3 - 4 tbsp of fat in the pan.

6. Place the pan back on a medium-high heat and allow to get hot. Add the duck breasts, 2 - 3 pieces at a time and brown for 3 - 5 minutes on each side, or until golden on both sides, gently pressing down with a spoon so that they caramelise evenly - depending on the thickness. It should remain pink inside.

7. Transfer the duck breasts to a warmed plate and put in a cool oven (90 °C / 190 °F / Gas mark ¼) to rest for 5 - 10 minutes.

8. To serve, thinly slice the duck breasts and arrange them on warm serving plates. Gently reheat the sauce for a few seconds and then spoon over the duck.

9. Sprinkle with a handful of pomegranate seeds before taking to the table.

Prepare ahead:

The sauce prepared up to the end of step 3 and the duck to the end of step 6 will keep well in the fridge for up to 2 days.

To use:

For the duck - remove the meat from the fridge a couple of hours before serving.

To warm the duck: either heat 1 tbsp of oil in a large non-stick frying pan over a medium heat, add the duck breasts and heat through for 1 - 2 minutes on each side, or briefly warm in a microwave for 1 - 2 minutes.

For the sauce:

Gently reheat the sauce, then spoon over the meat.

TIPS:

- You may replace the turmeric with ½ tsp ground saffron or 1 tsp saffron threads dissolved in 2 tbsp hot water.
- When reheating the sauce, if it is too thick you may need to add a further 1 - 2 tbsp of pomegranate juice.
- The duck fat incorporated in the olive oil will enhance the flavour of the dish.
- The reduced pomegranate juice gives a more intense flavour to the dish.

Warm Chilli Duck Breast Salad

This elegant salad with its vivid colours is delicious served with oven-roasted baby potatoes - see page 77.

For a buffet party, this recipe can easily be quadrupled.

The recipe for this dish is more or less the same as the chilli duck breast wraps in Easy and Elegant Dips, Canapés and Light Bites, page 89, but with no pancakes. You just need to add a couple of extra ingredients.

As a main course, it serves 2; as starter, it serves 4 - 5.

For the duck breasts:

Marinade and cook the duck breasts as instructed in Easy and Elegant Dips, Canapés and Light Bites – see page 89.

For the dressing:

Juice of 1 orange
25 ml (1 fl oz) mild olive oil
1 tbsp cider vinegar, to taste

Small piece of fresh ginger, peeled and grated, about ½ tsp, to taste
Salt and pepper

For the salad:

2 handfuls of baby leaf salad
½ cucumber, deseeded and finely chopped.

5 spring onions, trimmed and shredded lengthways
2 - 3 tbsp chopped fresh coriander

To garnish:

2 tbsp toasted sesame seeds and an orange cut into wedges

1. First make the dressing. In a small bowl, whisk together the orange juice, olive oil, cider vinegar and ginger. Season to taste.
2. After the duck has been roasted, remove from the oven. Allow to cool for 3 - 4 minutes before discarding the skins.
3. Thinly slice the meat and toss in the juices left from the cooking.
4. In a large bowl, mix all the salad ingredients.
5. Place a handful of salad on each plate and then arrange a few duck slices on top. Sprinkle with the toasted sesame seeds and arrange the orange wedges around the edge of the plate.
6. Before taking to the table, warm the dressing and pour over the salad.

Prepare ahead:

You may use either of these TWO options:

1. Prepare the duck salad to the end of step 4 a couple of hours in advance, loosely cover with cling film and store in a cool place. When ready to serve, place a non-stick frying pan over a high heat. Once it is very hot, place the duck slices with their juices in the pan and very briefly heat through for 20 - 30 seconds on each side.
    Then continue from step 5.

2. Make the dressing to the end of step 1. Prepare the duck to the end of step 3 then chill, cover and refrigerate for up to 1 day. When ready to serve, prepare the salad as in step 4 and then very briefly heat through the duck slices.
    Next carry out step 5.

Beef in a Richly Tomato-flavoured Bean Sauce with Crispy Bread Crumbs, Gruyere & Rosemary Topping

This is the ultimate meal in a pot. Tasty, economical and great for feeding lots of people. All it needs as an accompaniment is a big bowl of mixed crunchy green salad.

Serves 5 - 7

2 tbsp olive oil

1 large onion, peeled and finely chopped

3 celery sticks, finely chopped

2 large carrots, peeled and finely chopped

600 g (1 lb 5 oz) best quality lean minced beef

2 large garlic cloves, peeled and crushed

1 tsp ground turmeric

½ tsp cinnamon

½ tsp smoked paprika or chilli powder (although the latter gives a less pronounced flavour to the dish)

1 x 400 g tin of chopped tomatoes

3 tbsp tomato purée

1 vegetable or chicken stock cube, soften in 3 tbsp water

1 medium tart cooking apple, about 300 g (11 oz) peeled and grated

1 x 400 g tin of mixed beans or 125 g (5 oz) dried beans soaked and cooked - see page 138

250 ml (9 fl oz) water

Dash of balsamic or cider vinegar

Salt and pepper

For the topping:

150 g (6 oz) fresh white bread crumbs

150 g (6 oz) Gruyere cheese, grated

1½ tsp dried rosemary

Dash of olive oil

Use a shallow baking dish, about 28 x 28 cm (11 x 11 in) or 30 x 25 cm (12 x 10 in)

1. Heat the oil in a large non-stick sauce pan on a medium-low heat and add the onion, celery and carrots. Lightly season with salt and pepper, stir well, then cover and cook for 5 - 6 minutes or until the vegetables starting to soften, stirring regularly.

2. Add the meat and cook over a medium-high heat until it starts to brown, stirring occasionally. Sprinkle over the garlic, turmeric, cinnamon, smoked paprika or chilli powder. Mix well and cook for another 1 - 2 minutes before adding the chopped tomatoes, tomato purée, vegetable stock or chicken stock, apple, beans, water and a dash of balsamic or cider vinegar. Season with salt and pepper, stir to combine then bring to the boil. Cover and simmer over a low heat for about 20 minutes until the mixture has thickened slightly. Taste and adjust the seasoning.

3. Heat the oven to 200 °C / 400 °F / Gas mark 6.

4. Mix the bread crumbs with cheese and rosemary.

5. Spoon the meat into the baking dish. Scatter the bread crumb mixture over the top of in a roughly even layer and drizzle with a little olive oil. Bake in the oven for 10 - 15 minutes or until is bubbling and golden brown.

Note:

To keep the dish warm at the end of step 5 for 50 - 60 minutes, cover and place it in a warm oven at (90 °C 190 °F / Gas mark ¼).

Prepare ahead:

Complete to the end of step 2, one day in advance. Chill, cover and refrigerate. Warm the meat mixture through before carrying out step 3.

Persian Style Meatballs with Coriander and Tomato Sauce & Oven Roasted Aubergine

Fragrantly spiced meatballs combined with aubergine and tomatoes. In this dish the recipe for the meatballs is the same as Persian style meatballs in the Easy and Elegant Dips, Canapés and Light Bites, page 93.
Serve with golden fluffy rice or couscous (see page 135) and a crispy green salad.
Serves 5

For the meatballs:

Make the recipe the same way as in the Easy and Elegant Dips, Canapés and Light Bites - see page 93 until the end of step 2.

For the vegetables:

1 medium aubergine, about 450 g (1 lb)	2 - 3 tbsp olive oil
1 red pepper, deseeded and roughly chopped	

For the tomato sauce:

2 tbsp olive oil	300 ml (½ pint) water
1 medium onion, peeled and finely chopped	Pinch of dried chilli flakes (optional)
2 fat garlic cloves, peeled and crushed	3 - 4 tbsp natural Greek yoghurt at room temperature
1 x 400 g tin of chopped tomato	Salt and pepper
1 tbsp tomato purée	

To garnish:

2 tbsp chopped fresh coriander
Pre-heat the oven to 220 °C / 425 °F / Gas mark 7.

1. Cut the aubergines into about 2½ cm (1 inch) cubes. Place the aubergines and pepper in a roasting tin, drizzle over the oil, lightly season with salt and pepper and toss to coat. Roast in the pre-heated oven for 20 - 25 minutes or until soft and golden. Turn the vegetables over half way during the cooking. Remove from the oven and set aside.
2. Meanwhile brown the meatballs - see page 93. Remove from the pan.

3. To make the tomato sauce, heat the 2 tbsp of oil in the same frying pan that the meatballs have been browned in, then add the onion and sauté over a medium heat until lightly golden and soft. Next add the garlic and cook for 30 - 35 seconds before stirring in the tomatoes, tomato purée, water and chilli flakes, if using.

4. Transfer the sauce into a saucepan. Bring to the boil, cover and simmer over a low heat for about 5 minutes.

5. Tip in the meatballs, stir gently, cover and cook for a further 15 - 20 minutes.

6. Finally add the roasted vegetables with their juices from the roasting tin. Lightly stir to bring everything together, cover and simmer over a low heat for a further 5 minutes. Remove from the heat.

7. Carefully stir in the yoghurt. Try not to stir too much or you will completely break up the aubergines. Taste and adjust the seasoning.

8. Transfer the meatballs into a serving dish and carefully spoon over the sauce and sprinkle with the coriander before taking to the table.

Note:

To keep the dish warm at the end of step 7 for 50 - 60 minutes, cover and place it in a warm oven (90 °C / 190 °F / Gas mark ¼).

Prepare ahead:

The dish prepared to the end of step 6, keeps well in the fridge for up to 1 day.

To use:

Follow from step 7.

Lightly Spiced Rustic Pie with Crusty Sweet Potato Topping

This delicious pie is always a welcome dish in any buffet.
Serve with couple of colourful salads such as cannellini, beetroot and apple (see page 143) and a crisp green salad.

Serves 5 - 6

2 - 3 tbsp olive oil

1 large onion, peeled and finely chopped

3 celery sticks, finely chopped

600 g (1 lb 5 oz) best quality lean
   minced beef or lamb

2 large garlic cloves, peeled and crushed

1 tsp ground turmeric

1 tsp mixed dried herbs or thyme

½ tsp smoked paprika or hot chilli
   powder (though the latter has less
   pronounced flavour)

300 g (11 oz) mixed frozen vegetables
   (a mix of carrots, peas and sweet corn)

1 x 400 g tin of chopped tomatoes

1 - 2 tbsp tomato purée, to taste

1 beef or chicken stock cube, soften in
   100 ml water

250 ml (9 fl oz) red wine (optional)

Salt and pepper

For the topping:

600 g (1 lb 5 oz) sweet potatoes, peeled
and finely chopped

600 g (1 lb 5 oz) all-purpose potatoes
such as King Edward, peeled and
finely chopped

2 - 3 tbsp oil

Handful of grated matured cheddar
cheese about 200 g (7 oz)

Salt and pepper

Use a shallow baking dish, about 28 x 28 cm (11 x 11 in) or 30 x 25 cm (12 x 10 in).

1. In a large saucepan, heat the oil and sauté the onion and celery until lightly golden. Then add the meat and cook over a medium-high heat until it starts to brown, stirring occasionally. Sprinkle over the turmeric, garlic, mixed herbs and smoked paprika or hot chilli powder. Mix well and cook for another 1 - 2 minutes.

2. Next add the mixed vegetables, chopped tomatoes, tomato purée, beef or chicken stock and wine - if using any. Season with salt and pepper, stir to combine, then bring to the boil. Cover and simmer over a low heat for about 20 minutes until the mixture has thickened slightly. Taste and adjust the seasoning.

3. Meanwhile pre-heat the oven to 220 °C / 425 °F / Gas mark 7.

4. Place the potatoes in a roasting tin and sprinkle over the oil and season with salt and pepper. Toss to coat. Roast in the pre-heated oven for about 20 minutes or until they are lightly golden brown and softened. Turn the potatoes over half way during the cooking. Remove from the oven.

5. Reduce the heat to 200 °C / 400 °F / Gas mark 6.

6. Spoon the meat into the oven dish. Top with the potatoes and even out the surface with a fork. Sprinkle over with the cheese. Bake in the oven for 5 - 10 minutes or until it is bubbling and golden brown.

Note:
To keep the dish warm at the end of step 6 for 50 - 60 minutes, cover it and place it in a warm oven about (90 °C / 190 °F / Gas mark ¼).

VARIATION
You may replace the wine with about 450 g (1 lb) tart apples, peeled, cored and grated. At the end of step 2, use a fork to stir the dish a few times to break up the apples. This adds a special piquancy to the sauce.

Prepare ahead:
Complete the dish to the end of step 4, one day in advance. Chill, cover and refrigerate.

To use:
Bring the potatoes to room temperature and reheat the meat before carrying out step 5.

Braised Pork / Lamb with Apples & White Beans

The sweet and sour earthy flavour of this dish just needs saffron rice (see page 132) and a bowl of lightly cooked green vegetables as accompaniments.

Serves 5

Lamb with apples

600 g (1 lb 5 oz) boneless pork loin steak, any excess fat removed and cut into bite-size cubes or 600 g (1 lb 5 oz) diced leg of lamb

3 tbsp olive oil

1 medium red onion, peeled and finely sliced

1 tsp turmeric

½ tsp cinnamon

2 tbsp tomato purée

3 tbsp cider vinegar

2 tbsp sugar

1 beef or chicken stock cube, softened in 3 tbsp water

500 ml (18 fl oz) water

2 medium tart cooking apples about 450 g (1 lb) peeled, cored and grated

1 tsp saffron threads or ½ tsp ground saffron (optional)

1 x 400 g tin of white beans, drained and rinsed - or 125 g (5 oz) dried beans, soaked and cooked - see page 138.

Salt and pepper

To garnish:

One large Cox's apple, unpeeled, cored, thinly sliced and briefly sautéed in a knob of butter.

1. In a large saucepan, heat the oil on a medium-low heat, add the onion and sauté until lightly golden and soften. Then add the pork or lamb, sprinkle with turmeric, cinnamon, salt and pepper and brown the meat. Stir in the tomato purée, cider vinegar, sugar, beef or chicken stock, water, apple and saffron, if using. Bring to the boil. Pop the lid on and simmer over a low heat for about 50 - 55 minutes for pork and 60 - 65 minutes for the lamb or until the meat is tender.

2. Add the beans, stir to combine. Bring to the boil. Cover and simmer over a low heat for another 10 - 15 minutes. Remove from the heat.

3. Use a fork to press the apples to break them up. This adds a special piquancy to the sauce. Season to taste.

4. Melt the butter in a frying pan and sauté the apple slices for a few seconds on each side.
5. Transfer the meat with the sauce into a dish and arrange the apple slices on the top.

Note:
To keep the dish warm at the end of step 3 for 50 - 60 minutes, cover it and place it in a warm oven at (90 °C / 190 °F / Gas mark ¼).

Prepare ahead:
The meat prepared to the end of step 1 keeps well in the fridge for up to1 day and in the freezer for up to 1 month.

To use:
Warm the meat mixture through before carrying out step 2.

Parmesan & Sage Meatballs with Chorizo Sauce

This dish with a Mediterranean flavour and its bright colour makes an ideal party food. It tastes even better if prepared 1 day in advance.
Serve with roasted sweet potato wedges - see page 150 and lightly cooked fine green beans.
Makes about 30 - 35 meatballs
Serves 5 - 6

2 - 3 tbsp olive oil
1 bunch spring onion, trimmed and
   finely chopped
500 g (1 lb 2 oz) best quality lean
   minced pork
100 g (4 oz) parmesan cheese

1 tbsp dried sage
¼ - ½ tsp cayenne pepper or hot chilli
   powder, to taste
1 tsp tomato purée
1 large egg lightly beaten
Salt and pepper

For the chorizo tomato sauce:

1 tbsp olive oil
150 g (6 oz) chorizo sausages,
   finely chopped

1 x 400 g tin of chopped tomatoes
250 ml (9 fl oz) water
Pinch of sugar

To garnish:
A small handful of shredded basil leaves

1. Heat 1 tbsp of oil in a frying pan on a medium heat, add the spring onions and cook for about 1 - 2 minutes until softened. Set aside to cool.
2. Place the ground meat, spring onions, parmesan cheese, sage, cayenne pepper, tomato purée and egg in a food processor. Season with salt and pepper and blend for a few seconds until the mixture becomes a paste. Wet your hands then shape the mixture into 30 - 35 walnut-sized balls.
3. Heat the remaining 1 - 2 tbsp of oil in a non-stick frying pan on a high heat. Add the meatballs and fry until evenly golden browned on the outside and transfer to a plate.

4. In the same pan, heat 1 tbsp oil. Add the chopped chorizos and cook over a medium-high heat for 2 - 3 minutes, stirring occasionally until it is golden and most of the fat has rendered out. Add the tomatoes, water and pinch of sugar and stir to combine.
5. Transfer the sauce into a saucepan. Bring to the boil, cover and simmer over a low heat for about 5 minutes. Tip in the meatballs, stir gently, cover and cook for a further 15 - 20 minutes. Taste and adjust the seasoning.
6. Garnish before taking to the table.

Note:
To keep the meatballs warm at the end of step 5 for 50 - 60 minutes, cover the dish and place it in a warm oven at (90 °C / 190 °F / Gas mark ¼).

Prepare ahead:
The meatballs prepared to the end of step 3 will keep in the fridge for up to 2 days or in the freezer for up to 1 month. And the same goes for the tomato and chorizo sauce prepared to the end of step 4.

To use:
Warm the sauce through before carrying out step 5.

VARIATION

At step 5, add 1 x 400 g white beans, which have been drained and rinsed, to the sauce along with the meatballs.

Quinoa with orange, avocado, fresh lime and ginger

Basmati rice

This is my favourite rice, with its unique flavour. It is versatile and makes a lovely accompaniment to most dishes. Basmati rice is very easy to cook if you keep these tried and tested tips.

TIPS:

- Wash the rice under cold running water until the water runs clear to get rid of most of the starch clinging to the grains and to avoid ending up with a pot of sticky, gelatinous rice. This will ensure perfect, fluffy rice.
- Remember that rice dishes carry on cooking after they have been removed from the heat, so factor this in.
- Rice is best served straight away. However, you may cover the dished-out rice and place in a warm oven at (90 °C / 190 °F / Gas mark ¼) for a couple of hours until ready to eat.
- If you have to prepare ahead of time, cool the rice quickly by using a fork to gently fluff it up and then spread it onto a cold platter. Chill, cover and keep in the fridge for up to 1 day. When required, either heat by using 1 - 2 tbsp of mild olive oil in a non-stick frying pan, add the rice and stir gently to heat through or cover the dish and briefly warm the rice in the microwave.

Persian Style Saffron Rice

Serves 4 - 5

Vegetarian

250 g (10 oz) basmati rice, washed, as above

500 ml (18 fl oz) cold water

¼ tsp ground saffron or 1 tsp saffron threads

Knob of butter or 2 - 3 tbsp sunflower oil

Salt

To garnish:

A handful of toasted flaked almonds (see page 136) - optional

1. In a large sauce pan, place the washed rice, water, saffron, butter or oil and a pinch of salt. Bring to the boil. Lightly stir, cover and simmer over a low heat for about 15 minutes or until the rice is just tender and all the water has been absorbed. Remove from the heat, take off the lid and cover the pan with a clean tea cloth for 5 minutes.
2. Gently fluff up the rice with a fork. Take a spatula full of rice at a time and place it on a serving platter.

3. Sprinkle with almonds, if using, before taking to the table.

Note:

To keep the rice warm at the end of step 2 for a couple of hours, cover the dish and place it in a warm oven (90 °C / 190 °F / Gas mark ¼).

Prepare ahead:

The rice prepared to the end of step 2 keeps well in the fridge for up to 1 day. To store and use - see page 132.

VARIATIONS

Fragrant Turmeric & Cinnamon Rice

Substitute the saffron with:

½ tsp of turmeric   2 - 3 crushed cardamoms (see page 66)
½ tsp of cinnamon   optional

1. In a large saucepan, heat the butter or oil. Add the turmeric and cinnamon and cook over a low heat for 30 - 40 seconds.
2. Add the washed rice, a pinch of salt and cardamom, if using. Gently turn the grains to coat with the spices. Next stir in the water and bring to the boil.
3. Cook the rice as instructed in recipe 1 in this section.

Fragrant Rice with Mint & Pomegranate Seeds

As above, but after fluffing up the rice, you may gently toss in a handful of pomegranate seeds and chopped fresh mint.

Oven Baked Mushroom & Chestnut Risotto

This delicious wholesome risotto is very easy to make and offers a quick alternative to the traditional way of preparation.

Serve with beetroot salsa (see page 159) and a bowl of mixed petits pois and fine green beans.

Serves 6 - 8

Vegetarian

125 g (5 oz) butter
1 medium onion, peeled and finely
  chopped

500 g (1 lb 2 oz) brown-cap
mushrooms, cleaned and roughly
chopped
350 g (13 oz) risotto rice, such as
Arborio or Carnaroli
2 vegetable stock cubes, dissolved in 3
tbsp water

1.2 litre (2 pints) hot water
300 ml (11 fl oz) ml dry sherry
1 tbsp dried thyme or mixed herbs
Salt and pepper
200 g (8 oz) vacuum packed chestnuts,
roughly chopped
100 g (4 oz) grated parmesan cheese

To garnish:

A handful of shredded wild rocket leaves. Lime wedges to serve.

Use an oven-proof dish - about 28 x 28 cm (11 x 11 in) or 30 x 25 cm (12 x 10 in).

1. Pre-heat the oven to 180 °C / 350 °F / Gas mark 4.
2. Melt the butter in a large non-stick saucepan on a medium heat. Add the onion and sauté for 4 - 6 minutes or until lightly golden, stirring regularly. Add the mushrooms and cook for another 2 - 3 minutes.
3. Then add the rice, vegetable stock, water, sherry and thyme. Bring to the boil and season with salt and pepper to taste.
4. Next spoon the rice mixture into the baking dish.
5. Cook uncovered in the oven for 35 - 40 minutes or until the rice has completely absorbed the liquid. Half way through the cooking, remove the dish from the oven, give it a gentle stir and return to the oven.
6. When the risotto is done, remove it from the oven and gently stir in the chopped chestnuts and 2/3 of the parmesan cheese. Adjust seasoning to taste.
7. Sprinkle the risotto with the remaining parmesan cheese and garnish with wild rocket leaves before taking to the table. Serve with lime wedges.

VARIATION

Saffron Risotto

Make the recipe in the same way. Just replace the sherry with white wine and add a pinch of ground saffron or saffron threads to the rice mixture in step 3.
You may also leave out the mushrooms and chestnuts.

Note:

You may prepare the dish to the end of step 6 a couple of hours in advance.
When ready to serve warm through in a pre-heated oven (200 °C / 400 °F / Gas mark 6) for about 5 - 7 minutes.

Prepare ahead:

The onion and mushrooms prepared to the end of step 2 keep well in the fridge for up to 2 days.

Note:

Chestnuts - vacuum packed whole cooked chestnuts are available in most supermarkets.

Couscous

This grain is very versatile. Here are three of my favourite recipes.

Persian Style Couscous with Pomegranate Seeds & Fresh Mint

You may serve this light dish cold. It keeps well in the fridge for up to 1 day.
Serves 4 - 5
Vegetarian

250 g (10 oz) couscous
2 tbsp olive oil
½ tsp each of ground turmeric and
   cinnamon
Handful of pomegranate seeds

Handful of fresh chopped mint
Handful of chopped pistachio is
   optional
Salt and pepper

1. Cook the couscous following the instructions on the packet. Then gently fluff up the couscous with a fork.
2. Heat the oil in a non-stick frying pan. Stir in the turmeric and cinnamon and cook over a low heat for 30 - 40 seconds. Add the couscous. Gently turn the grains to coat with the spices. Remove from the heat and season with salt and pepper to taste.
3. Transfer into a serving dish and mix with the pomegranate seeds, chopped mint and pistachio, if using.

Note:

To keep the couscous warm at the end of step 2 for a couple of hours, cover the dish and place it in a warm oven (90 °C / 190 °F / Gas mark ¼).

Prepare ahead:

The couscous prepared to the end of step 2 keeps well in the fridge for up to two days. You may warm the couscous through briefly in a microwave for 1 - 2 minutes before carrying out step 3.

VARIATIONS

Persian Style Couscous with toasted pine nuts

Make the recipe in the same way; replace the pomegranate seeds and fresh mint with a handful of toasted pine nuts.

Saffron Couscous with Toasted Flaked Almonds

Make the recipe in the same way and just add:

1. A knob of melted butter, about 50 g (2 oz) and a pinch of ground saffron or saffron threads to the water used for cooking the couscous at the beginning of step 1.
2. Gently fluff up the cooked saffron couscous, and toss in a handful of toasted almond flakes (about 50 g / 2 oz). Season with salt and pepper to taste.

Quinoa

Quinoa (pronounced keen-wa) is an ancient grain which was referred to by the Incas as the mother of all grains. It has a pleasant texture and contains 18 per cent more protein than any other grains, is gluten-free, easy to cook and excellent for those with wheat-intolerance. This wholesome grain has a lovely texture and can be used as a substitute for rice or couscous.

Here I share with you two of my favourite recipes.

Quinoa with Aduki Beans Salsa

This dish is substantial enough to be served to vegetarian friends as a main course. Serve with cantaloupe melon with cucumber and fresh mint dressing and a Waldorf salad - see pages 158, 159. A smoked chicken and mango salad (see page 119) can be served with it to please non-vegetarian friends too.

You may serve this dish warm or at room temperature.

Serves 10 - 12

Vegetarian

For the salsa:

1 x 400 g tin of Aduki beans, drained and well rinsed or 125 g (5 oz) of dried Aduki beans, soaked and cooked - see page 139.

5 spring onions, trimmed and finely chopped

2 - 3 medium tomatoes, deseeded and finely chopped

1 yellow pepper, deseeded and finely chopped

1 red chilli, deseeded and finely chopped

½ tsp cumin

Dash of fresh lime juice

2 tbsp olive oil

Salt and pepper

For the quinoa:

200 g (8 oz) quinoa

400 ml (14 fl oz) water

2 - 3 tbsp olive oil

1 tsp ground turmeric

100 g (4 oz) currants, washed

1 tsp ground cinnamon

Salt and pepper

Small handful of chopped fresh mint or coriander optional

1. First make the salsa. Place the beans in a large bowl and mix with the rest of the salsa ingredients. Season with salt and pepper to taste and set aside.
2. Put the quinoa in a fine mesh strainer and rinse until the water runs clear. Then place in a saucepan with the 400 ml (14 fl oz) of cold water. Bring to the boil. Cover and simmer over a low heat for 15 - 20 minutes until the quinoa is just tender and all the water has been absorbed. Remove from the heat and with a fork gently fluff up the quinoa.
3. Heat the oil in a large frying pan. Add the turmeric and cook over a medium heat for 30 seconds before tossing in the currants and cinnamon. Cook for another 40 - 50 seconds. Then add the quinoa, gently turn the grains to coat with the spices. Remove from the heat.
4. Finally toss in the bean salsa and herb. Mix well and season to taste.

Note:
To keep the quinoa warm at the end of step 3 for 50 - 60 minutes, cover it and place it in a warm oven (90 °C / 190 °F / Gas mark ¼).

Prepare ahead:
This dish keeps well in the fridge for up to 2 days. Add the fresh mint or coriander just before serving.

Note:
You may cook quinoa in large quantities. Divide the plain cooked quinoa into small batches and store in the fridge for up to 3 days or in the freezer for up to 1 month.

Variation

Quinoa with Orange, Avocado, Fresh Lime & Ginger

This dish has a lovely refreshing oriental flavour. It keeps well in the fridge for up to 1 day. The avocado should be added just before serving.
Serves 5 - 7

For the salad:

200 g (8 oz) quinoa cooked in the same way as in step 2 of recipe 1 in this section

1 large ripe avocado

Dash of lime juice

2 oranges, peeled and finely diced

6 spring onions, trimmed and finely chopped

5 - 6 radishes, trimmed and finely chopped

For the dressing:

1 tbsp sesame oil or 1 - 1½ tbsp toasted sesame seeds.

3 tbsp sunflower oil

Dash of lime juice

2½ cm (1 in) piece of fresh ginger, peeled and grated, about 1 tsp, to taste

Dash of soy sauce

To garnish:

Salad cress

1. First make the dressing. In a small bowl, mix all the ingredients for the dressing and any orange juice from your cutting board. Season to taste and set aside.
2. Halve the avocado, remove the stone, peel and cut the flesh into bite-size chunks. Then gently toss the avocado in a dash of lime juice to delay browning.
3. In a large bowl, mix all the salad ingredients together. Drizzle over the dressing and gently mix. Season to taste and garnish with salad cress.

Pulses and Dried Beans

Beans are nourishing. Dishes made from pulses have a rather earthy charm with a comforting quality about them. They are very simple to prepare and cook.

To begin, all pulses are best digested if they are properly soaked before cooking and it is well worth taking extra care with the preparation, as follows:

1. Wash the beans; cover them with twice their volume of cold water and leave to soak overnight.
2. Then rinse the beans thoroughly under cold running water.
3. Place the pulses into a saucepan, cover with cold water and boil uncovered over a high heat for 10 - 15 minutes, skimming off any foam that rises to the surface.
4. Cover and cook over a medium heat until they soft, stirring regularly.

TIPS:

- Be aware that pulses do not keep indefinitely. Once the sell-by date has passed, they start to harden and sometimes no amount of cooking will soften them. So, always check dates.
- If you are concerned about the digestibility of beans such as chick peas, kidney beans, pinto beans, cannellini beans, etc., then after they have been boiled for 10 minutes, drain, rinse again under cold running water and then cook.
- If soaking beans overnight is not convenient, you may give them a short hot soak.

For this method:

1. Put the washed beans into a saucepan, cover with plenty of cold water, bring to the boil and simmer over a high heat for 15 minutes.
2. Remove from the heat, cover and leave to soak for about 2 - 3 hours depending on the type of beans or pulses.
3. Then drain and rinse under cold running water before carrying on cooking.

TIPS:

- Adding a piece of Kombu (a sea vegetable, available in most supermarkets) to the water during the cooking helps pulses become more digestible.
- Do not add salt or salty stock to the water because it hardens the skins of pulses and prevents them cooking properly.
- Acids such as lemon juice, vinegar and tomatoes have a similar effect on pulses. They are best added at the end of cooking.

Aduki (Azuki) Beans

These tiny reddish-brown beans with a nutty sweet flavour give colour and texture to rice and quinoa. They are also delicious in salads, soups and casseroles.

Chick peas

Chick peas are nutty and slightly crunchy, with very little flavour. To bring the best out of the chick peas in a salad, for example, toss them in warm vinaigrette dressing so that they absorb other favours.

Cooking times for beans and pulses

Cooking times vary a great deal, depending on the type of pulse and how old they are. As a rough guide, use the following times:

Aduki (Azuki) beans	30 - 35 minutes
Black eye beans	55 - 65 minutes
Cannellini beans	55 - 65 minutes
Pinto or kidney beans	65 - 75 minutes
Chick peas	65 - 85 minutes
Mixed beans	65 - 85 minutes

The best guide, of course, is to follow the cooking time given on the packet.

Measurement conversion

1 x 400 g tin = 250 g (10 oz) of drained cooked beans = 125 g (5 oz) dried beans.

Storing cooked beans

It is well worth cooking the whole pack of beans and then dividing into small batches. Pulses covered in a container keep well in the fridge for 4 - 5 days or in the freezer for up to 2 - 3 months.

Aduki Beans Salsa

Serves 6 - 8
Vegetarian

> 2 x 400 g tins of Aduki beans, drained
> and well rinsed or 250 g (10 oz) dried
> Aduki beans, soaked and cooked - see
> page 139.
> 1 medium red onion, peeled, finely
> chopped
> 2 - 3 medium tomatoes, finely chopped
> 1 yellow pepper, deseeded and finely
> chopped
> 1 chilli, deseeded and finely chopped
> Juice of 1 fresh lime
> 2 - 3 tbsp olive oil
> ½ tsp ground cumin
> Small handful of chopped fresh
> coriander or fresh mint
> Salt and pepper

In a large bowl, gently mix all the ingredients together and then season to taste.

Prepare ahead:
This salad keeps well in the fridge for up to 2 days. Add the fresh herb just before serving.

VARIATION

Aduki Beans Salsa with Avocado

Halve one large ripe avocado. Remove the stone, peel and cut into bite-size chunks. Then gently toss the avocado in a dash of olive oil and lemon juice to delay browning. Add to the salsa just before serving.

Warm Chick Peas with Tomato & Coriander Salsa

This Middle Eastern salad is delicious served with a dollop of natural yoghurt, crisp lettuce and saffron rice or couscous - see pages 132, 135.

Serves 6 - 7
Vegetarian

> 2 - 3 tbsp olive oil
> 1 red chilli, deseeded and finely chopped
> or a pinch of dried chilli flakes
> 2 garlic cloves, peeled and crushed

Grated zest of 1½ lemon
Juice of 1 lemon

2 x 400 g tins of chick peas, drained and well rinsed or 250 g (10 oz) dried chicken peas, soaked and cooked

Salt and pepper

For the salsa:

1 small red onion peeled and finely chopped

½ cucumber, deseeded and finely chopped

3 - 4 medium tomatoes, deseeded and chopped

To garnish:

A small handful of chopped fresh coriander

1. In a large saucepan, mix the oil, chilli, garlic, lemon zest and lemon juice. Warm up the dressing over a low heat. Then add the chick peas and cook for 1 - 2 minutes.
2. Next transfer the beans to a bowl and leave to marinade for couple of hours to absorb the flavour.
3. Meanwhile mix together all the ingredients for the salsa in a bowl and set aside.
4. When ready to serve, warm the chick peas, then toss in the salsa and the herb. Season to taste and garnish.

Note:

You may replaced the coriander with shredded basil leaves

Prepare ahead:

The chick peas prepared to the end of step 2 keep well in the fridge for up to 3 days. The salsa prepared at step 3 keeps well in the fridge for up to 2 days. Add the fresh coriander or basil just before serving.

Roast Sweet Potatoes with Lightly Spiced Chick Peas

Sweet potatoes and chick peas make an interesting combination of texture and flavours which are enhanced by spices.

Serves 7 - 8

Vegetarian

1200 g (2lbs 10 oz) sweet potatoes, peeled and cut into small cubes, about 2½ cm (1 in)

4 - 5 tbsp olive oil

1 medium red onion, peeled and finely sliced

2 garlic cloves, peeled and crushed

1 red chilli deseeded, and finely chopped or a pinch of dried chilli flakes

2½ cm (1 in) piece of fresh ginger, peeled and grated, about 1 - 1½ tsp, to taste

½ tsp cinnamon

2 x 400 g tins of chick peas, drained and well rinsed or 250 g (10 fl oz) dried

chick peas, soaked and cooked - see page 138.

Juice of ½ - 1 fresh lime, to taste

75 g (3 oz) cherry tomatoes cut in half

Salt and pepper

To garnish:

A handful of chopped fresh mint, or chopped coriander

1. Pre-heat the oven to 200 °C / 400 °F / Gas mark 6.
2. Place the sweet potatoes in a large roasting tin, mix with 2 - 3 tbsp of oil and season with salt and pepper. Spread the potato cubes out and roast in the oven for 20 - 25 minutes or until crisp and beginning to soften. Turn the potatoes over half way during the cooking. When cooked, transfer them to a bowl and set aside.
3. Meanwhile heat the remaining 2 tbsp of the oil in a non-stick saucepan. Add the onion and sauté over a medium heat until lightly golden brown. Sprinkle over the garlic, chilli, ginger and cinnamon. Cook for 30 - 40 seconds before adding the chick peas and lime juice. Mix well, then cover and simmer over a low heat for 2 - 3 minutes to let the beans warm up in the onion mixture and absorb the flavour.
4. Add the potatoes and tomatoes. Stir gently. Cover and simmer for a further 2 - 3 minutes. Remove from the heat. Season to taste and garnish before taking to the table.

Note:

To keep the dish warm at the end of step 4 for 50 - 60 minutes, cover it and place it in a warm oven (90 °C / 190 °F / Gas mark ¼).

Prepare ahead:

The roasted sweet potatoes keep well in the fridge for up to 1 day and the chick peas prepared to the end of step 3 keep well in the fridge for up to 2 days.

VARIATION

You may substitute the chick peas with Cannellini beans, sweet potatoes with butternut squash and fresh chilli with ¼ tsp cayenne pepper.

Spicy Cannellini Beans & Chorizo

The piquancy of chorizo adds extra flavour to the beans. You may serve this dish warm or at room temperature.

Serves 3 - 5 as part of a selection.

100 g (4 oz) chorizo sausages, finely chopped

1 tbsp olive oil

1 x 400 g tin of Cannellini beans, drained and well rinsed or 125 g (5 oz)

dried Cannellini beans soaked and cooked - see page 138.

1 small red onion, peeled and finely chopped

150 g (6 oz) cherry tomatoes, cut into half

Dash of lime juice or balsamic vinegar   Salt and black pepper

To garnish:

A handful of chopped fresh parsley

1. Heat the oil in a frying pan. Add the chorizos and cook over a high heat for 2 - 3 minutes, until the chorizos turn golden and start to become crisp.
2. Add the beans, cover and simmer over a low heat for 2 - 3 minutes until warm through.
3. Next add the cherry tomatoes, onion and a dash of lime juice or balsamic vinegar. Lightly stir to bring everything together. Season to taste.
4. Transfer to a serving dish and sprinkle over the chopped parsley.

Prepare ahead: The beans prepared to the end of step 2, keep well in the fridge for up 2 days.
To use: Warm the beans through before starting step 3.

Cannellini, Beetroot & Apple Salad

A strong contrast of colours is a special feature of this tasty salad.
Serves 4 - 5
Vegetarian

For the dressing:

5 tbsp olive oil   Dash of balsamic vinegar

2 tbsp lemon juice

For the salad:

1 x 400 g tin of Cannellini beans,   2 medium granny Smith apples
  drained and well rinsed or 125 g (5 oz)   3 celery sticks, trimmed
  dried Cannellini beans soaked and   4 spring onions, trimmed
  cooked - see page 138   1 x 250 g (10 oz) pack ready cooked and
2 - 3 tbsp dry cranberries or raisins,   peeled beetroot
  washed   Salt and pepper

1. First make the dressing. In a large bowl, mix the oil, lemon juice, a dash of balsamic vinegar and a pinch of salt and pepper.
2. Then toss in the beans and cranberries or raisins. Mix well and set aside for 20 - 30 minutes to absorb the flavour.
3. Finely chop the apples, celery sticks, spring onions and beetroot. Add to the beans and mix well. Season to taste

Prepare ahead:
The salad keeps well in the fridge for up to 1 day.

Potato and broccoli frittata

Versatile Vegetables

Vegetables are full of flavour and nutrients, add interest and colour to meals and are a necessary component to almost any meal. To bring out the best in vegetables during cooking, consider different ways of cooking them.

Try different vegetables in different ways - roasting, sweating or sautéing vegetables for different flavours and textures.

Aubergines (aka Eggplants)

To enjoy the full flavour of this lovely versatile vegetable, keep these notes in mind.

To prepare: Large, fat aubergines might taste slightly bitter. To remove the bitterness, fill a large pot with cold water and add 2 - 3 tbsp of salt to it. Tip in the sliced / chopped aubergines and leave for 30 - 35 minutes, stirring occasionally. Then drain. Pat dry the aubergines or place them in a colander to dry for couple of hours or overnight in the fridge.

To cook: Aubergines with their soft flesh tend to soak up oil. To cook with the minimum oil place a frying pan on a high heat. Once the pan is hot, add the oil. If the oil is not hot, it will soak into the flesh. Then toss the aubergine chunks / slices into the hot oil. If unpeeled, make sure the flesh side is facing down. Cover and cook over a high heat for 4 - 5 minutes or until light golden brown. Remove the lid and turn the aubergines over. Then cover and cook for a further 3 - 5 minutes until caramelised and the flesh becomes soft.

TIP:

- Brushing both sides of the aubergine slices with beaten egg white reduces the oil needed for frying.

Peppers

Red, yellow and orange peppers have sweeter flavour than green pepper. I like to use them for roasting.

Potatoes

My favourite potatoes are King Edwards, Red Booster, Maris Piper, Wilja, Desiree and Green Vale because they are suitable for all purposes.

To roast vegetables:

- Slice the vegetables uniformly to cook evenly.
- Heat the oil in a large roasting tin in a hot oven for 4 - 5 minutes until sizzling hot.

- Then toss in the seasoned vegetables and mix to thoroughly coat with the oil. (Tossing the vegetables in hot oil will release their natural sugars and allow them to colour and caramelise.)
- Stir gently only once half way through cooking to prevent too much browning on one side.

Sweated vegetables consume less oil and also make a delicate sweet base for most dishes.

To sweat vegetables:
- Heat a little oil or mixture of oil and butter in a pan and add the vegetables.
- Lightly season, then cover and cook over a low heat for a few minutes, stirring occasionally.
- Keeping the lid on the pan while cooking helps the vegetables to steam in their own juices.

To sauté vegetables:
Cook the vegetables in a little oil or a mixture of oil and butter, over a medium / high heat for a few minutes, stirring often until lightly golden brown.

TIPS:

- Vegetables diced into small pieces cook quickly and are best for soups and sauces, whilst larger chunks are better for casseroles and stews.
- Vegetables, particularly onions, sautéed in small quantities caramelise better.
- Before peeling, soak onions in cold water for 20 - 30 minutes as this will reduce or stop your eyes watering when you chop them.
- Stock cubes - I use Knorr or Kallo organic stock cubes for stock.

Mediterranean Roasted Vegetables with Saffron & Chestnuts

served with fresh herb crème fraiche

This dish with its lovely sweet and intense flavour can be served either hot or at room temperature as a vegetarian main course.

Serves about 6 as a main course, 7 - 9 as a side dish

Vegetarian

300 g (11 oz) sweet potatoes, peeled and cut into about 5 cm (2 in) chunks

300 g (11 oz) baby potatoes left unpeeled and cut into about 2½ cm (1 in) cubes

2 medium red onions, peeled and cut into quarters

350 g (11 oz) courgette trimmed and cut into bite-sized pieces

300 g (11 oz) aubergine left unpeeled, trimmed and cut into about 5 cm (2 in) cubes

2 red peppers, deseeded and roughly chopped

6 tbsp olive oil

¼ tsp ground saffron or 1 tsp saffron threads dissolved in 2 tbsp hot water

1 tsp dried thyme or dried mixed herbs

2 garlic cloves, peeled and crushed

200 g (8 oz) cooked chestnuts, roughly
chopped

Salt and pepper

For the sauce:

200 ml (7 fl oz) light crème fraiche or
natural Greek yoghurt

2 garlic cloves, peeled and crushed

1 tbsp freshly chopped parsley

Salt and pepper

1. Pre-heat the oven to 220 °C / 425 °F / Gas mark 7.
2. Place the vegetables in a large roasting tin. Add the oil, saffron, thyme and crushed garlic. Lightly season with salt and pepper and toss to coat.
3. Then cook for 35 - 40 minutes or until they are soft and golden. Turn the vegetables over half way during the cooking.
4. Meanwhile in a bowl, mix the crème fraiche or yoghurt, garlic and parsley. Season to taste and set aside.
5. Remove the vegetables from the oven.
6. Transfer into a serving dish and scatter the chestnuts over the top. Serve with the sauce.

Note:

To keep the vegetables warm at the end of step 5 for 30 - 40 minutes, cover it and place it in a warm oven (90 °C / 190 °F / Gas mark ¼).

Prepare ahead:

The vegetables prepared at the step 2 keep well in the fridge for up to 1 day. Bring the vegetables to room temperature, before carrying out step 3.

Variation

Make the recipe in the same way. Just leave out the saffron and thyme.

Note:

Chestnuts - vacuum packed whole cooked chestnuts are available in most supermarkets.

Char-Grilled Vegetables with Crispy Melting Feta

In this light and elegant dish, the vegetables are marinated in olive oil, and fresh lime juice with a hint of garlic for that extra bite.

Serves 5 - 6 as a side dish

Vegetarian

4 - 5 tbsp olive oil

2 tbsp fresh lime juice

2 - 3 courgettes about 600 g (1 lb 5 oz),
trimmed and cut into about 2½ cm
(1 in) slices

1 fat garlic clove, peeled and crushed

1 aubergine about 350 g (11 oz), left
unpeeled and cut into 2½ cm (1 in)
slices.

For the topping:

4 - 5 medium firm tomatoes, finely sliced, about 1¼ cm (½ in) thick

About 200 g (7 oz) feta cheese thinly sliced.

(You need one slice of tomato and one slice of feta cheese for each piece of vegetable)

Salt and pepper

1. Pre-heat the grill.
2. In a large bowl, mix the olive oil, lime juice and garlic. Add the aubergine and courgettes, lightly season with salt and pepper and toss to coat.
3. Spread the vegetables out in a large oven proof dish and grill for 7 - 10 minutes on each side or until lightly golden and beginning to soften. Remove from the oven.
4. Place one slice of tomato on each piece of vegetable and top with a slice of feta cheese. Return to the oven and grill for 4 - 5 minutes, until lightly golden brown.

VARIATION

Char-Grilled Vegetables with Tahini

Leave out the tomatoes and feta cheese. Add 2 tablespoons of tahini (see Note 2 below) to the olive oil, lime juice and garlic. Then make the recipe in the same way until the end of step 3.

Prepare ahead:

You may use either of these two options:

1. Grill the vegetables 2 - 3 hours in advance and serve them at room temperature.
2. Prepare the vegetables to the end of step 2, one day in advance. Cover and refrigerate. Bring them to room temperature before carrying out step 3.

Note:

1. You also may leave out the tahini.
2. Tahini is made from crushed roasted sesame seeds blended with sesame oil.

Oven Roasted Tomatoes with Crusty Herb & Parmesan

This incredibly simple dish is very pleasing. It has also the advantage of being able to be made a couple of hours in advance and served at room temperature.

For a stunning vegetable platter, lay the crusty-topped tomatoes on a large platter with char-grilled courgette, aubergine and feta - see page 147, and some al dente steamed asparagus.

Serves 5 - 7 as part of the vegetable platter

Vegetarian

5 medium firm tomatoes	2 tsp dried thyme
50 g (2 oz) white fresh bread crumbs	5 - 6 tbsp olive oil
4 tbsp parmesan cheese	Salt and pepper

1. Pre-heat the oven to 220 °C / 425 °F / Gas mark 7.
2. With a sharp knife, cut a very fine slice from the top and base of the tomatoes so that they can sit firm on the tray. Then cut the tomatoes in half.
3. In a bowl, mix the bread crumbs, parmesan and herbs. Then add enough olive oil to make it into a light crumbly paste. Taste and adjust the seasoning.
4. Top each tomato half with a spoon of the crumbs mixture.
5. Brush the base of a large oven proof tray with 1 tbsp of olive oil and heat in the oven for 2 - 3 minutes as this gives a nice crisp base to the tomatoes. Then place the tomatoes on the heated tray and cook for 8 - 10 minutes or until lightly golden brown. Remove from the oven and serve.

Note:

Do not leave the tomatoes on the hot tray for too long, as they will overcook.

Prepare ahead:

The crumbs prepared in step 3 keep well in the fridge for up to 3 days. Bring to room temperature before use. You may prepare the tomatoes to the end of step 4, three hours in advance. Twenty minutes before serving, carry out step 5.

VARIATIONS

Oven Roasted Tomatoes with Crusty Herb, Parmesan & Avocado

1. Make the recipe in the same way.
2. Halve one large ripe avocado. Remove the stone, peel and cut into bite-size chunks.
3. Then gently toss the avocado in a dash of olive oil and lemon juice to delay browning. Scatter the avocado chunks over roasted tomatoes before serving.

Oven Roasted Tomatoes with Crusty Herb, Bacon & Parmesan

Grill 2 rashers of bacon until crisp. Finely chop and add to the crumb mixture in step 3.

Smoked Paprika Roasted Sweet Potatoes Wedges

This is one of my favourite finger foods to serve with drinks. A pinch of smoked paprika adds just a little smokiness to the lovely sweetness of the potato.

Serve either hot or at room temperature with Persian style mint yoghurt - see page 71 - or sour cream.

Serves 4 when part of a main course, but 6 - 8 when served as finger food

4 sweet potatoes about 180 g (6 oz) each

4 - 5 tbsp olive oil

1 tsp smoked paprika

Salt

1. Pre-heat oven to 200 °C / 400 °F / Gas mark 6.
2. Cut the potatoes with the skins left on into chips roughly 5 x 2½ cm (2 x 1 in) thick.
3. Place the potatoes in a large roasting tin. Drizzle with the oil. Add the smoked paprika, lightly season with salt and toss to coat.
4. Spread the potatoes out and roast in the oven for 15 minutes. Turn the potatoes over and continue roasting until crisp and beginning to soften (about 10 - 15 minutes).

Prepare ahead:

You may use either of these two options:

A.

Roast the potatoes up to 2 - 3 hours in advance. When ready to serve, reheat for 3 - 4 minutes in a pre-heated oven (200 °C / 400 °F / Gas mark 6).

B.

Prepare the potatoes up to the end of step 3, four to five hours in advance. Then, a little while before serving, place the potatoes in the preheated oven.

VARIATION

Roasted Sweet Potato Wedges

Make the recipe in the same way. Just leave out the smoked paprika.

Petits Pois and Sugar Snap Peas with Lime, Honey & Mustard Dressing

Serves 4 - 5 as side dish

Vegetarian

For the dressing:

4 tbsp olive oil

Juice of ½ a lime

½ - 1 tsp whole grain mustard

1 tsp runny honey

Small handful of fresh tarragon finely chopped

Salt and pepper

For the vegetables:

350 g (13 oz) fresh or frozen petits pois

200 g (8 oz) sugar snap peas

1. First make the dressing. In a large bowl, whisk together the olive oil, lime juice, mustard, honey and tarragon. Season with salt and pepper to taste and set aside.
2. Cook the petits pois in boiling lightly salted water for 3 - 4 minutes for fresh peas and 2 - 3 minutes for frozen. Then drain.
3. Cook the sugar snap peas in boiling, lightly salted water for 2 - 3 minutes. Then drain.
4. In a large bowl, toss all the vegetables in the dressing while they are still warm.

Asparagus and Petits Pois with Toasted Hazelnuts

Serves 3 - 4 as side dish
Vegetarian

1 bunch of asparagus	Grated zest of 1 lemon
350 g (13 oz) fresh or frozen petits pois	2 tbsp of roughly chopped toasted
1 knob of butter	hazelnuts

1. Remove the woody stems from the asparagus by bending the end of spear. They should snap easily at the point where the woody part begins.
2. Lightly cook the asparagus in boiling lightly salted water for about 3 - 4 minutes, then drain.
3. Cook the petits pois in boiling lightly salted water for 3 - 4 minutes for fresh peas and 2 - 3 minutes for frozen, then drain.
4. Melt the butter in a non-stick frying pan. Add the cooked asparagus, petits pois and lemon zest. Stir well and season to taste. Remove from the heat.
5. Transfer into a serving dish and sprinkle with the toasted hazelnuts.

French beans & Petits Pois with a Tarragon Dressing

The fresh chopped tarragon adds a refreshing lift to this side dish.
Serves 5 - 7
Vegetarian

For the dressing:

6 tbsp olive oil	½ tsp Dijon Mustard
2 tbsp cider vinegar	Pinch of sugar
1 - 1½ tbsp fresh tarragon leaves, roughly chopped	Salt and pepper

For the vegetables:

300 g (11 oz) petits pois	350 g (13 oz) French beans, trimmed and cut into bite-size pieces

1. First make the dressing. In a large bowl, whisk together the olive oil, vinegar, tarragon, mustard and sugar. Season to taste.

2. Cook the petits pois in boiling lightly salted water and drain
3. Lightly cook the French beans in boiling, lightly salted water and drain.
4. Toss the vegetables in the dressing while still warm.

Persian Style Frittata

Frittatas are versatile Italian omelettes, hence the name. They are somewhat similar to Spanish tortilla. These two - Broccoli and Potato Frittata and Spinach Frittata - are Persian style and make ideal party food, particularly for vegetarian friends.

Cut them into small wedges and serve with refreshing Carrot & Cucumber Salsa or couple of inviting salads such as Waldorf salad, Carrot, Chilli and Coconut Salad (see pages 162, 159, 161). Frittatas can be prepared a day in advance and they are delicious served at room temperature - see Note below.

Note:
For a finger buffet, you may cut the frittata into small squares. These recipes make about 28 - 30 pieces.

Broccoli & Potato Frittata

Serves 5 - 7
Vegetarian

2 large potatoes, about 450 g (1 lb) such as Charlotte or other waxy potatoes

6 - 7 tbsp mild olive oil

1 large onion, peeled and finely chopped

1 tsp curry powder

250 g (10 oz) broccoli, lightly cooked and finely chopped

6 large eggs

1 tbsp self-raising flour (optional)

½ tsp baking powder

Salt and pepper

Use an oven-proof dish - about 28 x 28 cm (11 x 11 in) or 30 x 25 cm (12 x 10 in)

1. Peel and dice the potatoes into small cubes, about 1¼ cm (½ in), and cook in lightly salted boiling water for 4 - 6 minutes or until just done, then drain in a colander.
2. Heat 3 tbsp of oil in a large non-stick frying pan and sauté the onion over a medium heat for 4 - 5 minutes or until lightly golden and soft. Stir in the curry powder and cook for 30 - 40 seconds before adding the potatoes and broccoli. To avoid the vegetables becoming too mushy, mix carefully. Remove from the heat and set aside to cool.
3. Meanwhile pre-heat the oven to 180 °C / 350 °F / Gas mark 4.
4. Break the eggs into a large bowl. Add the flour and baking powder. Beat thoroughly with a fork. Add the vegetable mixture and carefully mix. Season to taste.
5. Pour the remaining 3 - 4 tbsp of oil into the oven-proof dish and place it in the oven for 4 - 5 minutes, until the oil is sizzling hot. (This gives a nice crisp base to your frittata). Remove the dish from the oven. Pour in the egg mixture. Smooth the top with a spoon.

Some of the oil will cover the surface. Bake uncovered for 45 - 50 minutes or until golden brown. Remove from the oven. Let it cool.

6.   Use a palette knife or fish slice to loosen the edges, and then cut the frittata into small wedges.

Note:

To store the baked frittata, cool, cover with a grease proof paper and foil before placing in the fridge.

To use:

Remove the frittata from the fridge 2 - 3 hours before serving. If you prefer to serve it warm, place the frittata in a hot oven (200 °C / 400 °F / Gas mark 6) for about 8 minutes.

Prepare ahead:

The potatoes and broccoli prepared to end of step 2 keep well in the fridge for up to 2 days. Bring the vegetables to room temperature before carrying out step 3.

Spinach Frittata

Serves 6 - 8

Vegetarian

     1 x 500 g (1 lb 2 oz) pack of frozen chopped spinach

     5 - 6 tbsp mild olive oil

     1 large onion, peeled and finely chopped

     6 large eggs, lightly beaten

     ½ tsp cinnamon

     1 tbsp self-raising flour (optional)

     1 tsp baking powder

     Handful of chopped walnuts (optional)

     Salt and pepper

Use an oven-proof dish -about 28 x 28 cm (11 x 11 in) or 30 x 25 cm (12 x 10 in)

1.   Place the frozen spinach in a saucepan and cook over a medium heat until thawed and all the moisture has evaporated. Aim for fairly dry spinach, otherwise the Frittata becomes soggy. Set aside the saucepan.

2. Heat 3 tbsp of oil in a frying pan. Sauté the onion over a medium heat for 4 - 5 minutes or until lightly golden and soft. Then add the spinach and cook over a high heat for 2 - 3 minutes. Transfer into a large bowl. Let it cool.

3. Meanwhile pre-heat the oven to 180 °C / 350 °F / Gas mark 4.

4. Add the eggs to the spinach mixture and mix well. Then add the cinnamon, flour, baking powder, walnuts - if using. Season with salt and pepper. Beat thoroughly with a fork. Taste and adjust the seasoning.

5. Pour 2 - 3 tbsp of oil into the ovenproof dish and place it in the oven for 4 - 5 minutes, until the oil is sizzling hot, which gives a nice crisp base to your frittata. Remove the dish from the oven and pour in the egg mixture. Smooth the top with a spoon. Some of the oil will cover the surface. Bake uncovered for 45 - 50 minutes, or until golden brown. Remove from the oven. Let it cool.

6. Use a palette knife or fish slice to loosen the edges and then cut the frittata into small wedges.

Note:

To store the baked frittata, cool, cover with a grease proof paper and foil before placing in the fridge.

To use:

Remove the frittata from the fridge 2 - 3 hours before serving. If you prefer to serve it warm, place the frittata in a hot oven (200 °C / 400 °F / Gas mark 6) for about 5 - 6 minutes.

Prepare ahead:

Spinach prepared to end of step 2 keeps well in the fridge for up to 2 day. Bring the spinach to room temperature before carrying out step 3.

Blueberry salad

Salads – Impressive and Easy Meals

Gorgeous salads appeal to all the senses. They are aromatic, full of fresh flavours and look beautiful on a plate. With all these temptations, they can bring a surge of excitement to the table, even in the company of simple dishes.

At times, tasty colourful salads are an excellent alternative to a cooked meal and demand very little of your time. With a dollop of imagination and a bit of know-how, you can transform commonplace salad ingredients into an elegant and appetizing creation on any budget.

What makes a salad impressive?

Body of the salad

The best way to create substantial salads is to choose one main ingredient and build complementary tastes, textures and colours around it. Protein foods such a cold, spiced chicken or roast beef make an excellent base for a salad, as do lighter ingredients such as mozzarella or prawns.

Soft foods, such as cold salmon, need the contrast of crunchy vegetables. Think balance. Sugar snap peas, broad beans, asparagus and crisp lettuce are the perfect partners to soft ingredients.

Taste

When choosing the base ingredients, try to balance the flavours with other items. Salty cheeses complement summer fruits such as pears, water melon or nectarines, whereas roast beef tastes amazing with either salty olives or anchovies. Salty and savoury ingredients such as capers, smoked salmon, crispy bacon pieces and parmesan add extra flavour. Also, capers add an extra touch scattered on cold roasted vegetables or into a potato salad.

Texture

To create a tempting salad, it helps to keep the dominant food texture quite similar, so that a salad might be crunchy, semi-soft or delicate. However, a light textured contrast such as crunchy bacon pieces or a soft-boiled egg can add interest.

Colour

Variety makes a salad look instantly attractive. After you have thought about the taste of the ingredients, think about what colours might look good together. For example, pale green crunchy sweet Romaine leaves can be offset with bright red sliced radishes or a little dark green rocket, whilst beetroot looks amazing with snipped chives and creamy white goat's cheese.

Toppings

Once you have three ingredients that enhance each another, add aromatic toppings such as sweet red onion, lemon zest, chives, mint, thyme, fennel, oregano, tarragon or basil, and leaves like watercress and rocket to excite the flavour. For example, a handful of toasted seeds / nuts, raisins, chopped dried apricots, some chopped avocadoes, or a few garlicky, herby croutons dusted with parmesan give a chic look and will enliven a plain green salad.

TIPS:

- Wash whole lettuces thoroughly because biting on grit spoils the pleasure of food. Once washed, make sure you dry the lettuce well. Wet leaves dilute taste and make salads lifeless. Either dry leaves with paper towels or invest in a salad spinner.
- To de-seed a cucumber, halve the cucumber lengthwise. Carefully remove the seeds with a spoon and then cut into the required size.
- To ripen avocado quicker, place in a paper bag with a banana which will give off ethanol, a gas that stimulates the ripening process. This applies to other fruits too.
- For maximum taste, use your salad ingredients at room temperature.
- Add the dressing just before serving and do not worry about garnishing. The chemistry between colours and textures is enough to reward all the senses.
- Use a roomy bowl with plenty of space to toss the salad well and cover all ingredients.
- To make a green salad more enticing, warm your salad dressing. Heat olive oil gently before adding mustard, vinegar and seasoning to bring out the flavours.
- For a tomato salad, use a flat plate to avoid overlapping slices which causes sogginess.

Salads

Spinach & Cranberry Salad with Toasted Hazelnuts & Balsamic Dressing

A salad with great flavour and dramatic colour.

Serves 5 - 7

Vegetarian

For the dressing:

5 tbsp olive oil	Pinch of sugar
2 tbsp balsamic vinegar	Salt and pepper
½ tsp Dijon Mustard	

For the salad:

50 g (2 oz) dried cranberries, washed	1 small red onion peeled and finely chopped
1 x 250 g (10 oz) bag fresh baby spinach leaves, washed and pat dried	2 large ripe dessert pears, cored, and cut into bite-size pieces
100 g (4 oz) toasted hazelnuts or cashew nuts, roughly chopped - see page 62.	

1. First make the dressing. Whisk together the olive oil, vinegar, mustard and sugar. Season with salt and pepper to taste.
2. In a small bowl, mix the cranberries with 2 tbsp of the dressing. Then set aside for 20 - 30 minutes to allow the cranberries to soften.
3. When ready to serve, place the spinach on a serving platter and arrange the pears, onion and half of the hazelnuts on top. Drizzle over the dressing. Then scatter cranberries and the rest of the hazelnuts over the salad.

Prepare ahead:

The dressing keeps well in the fridge for up to 3 days. Remove from the refrigerator 2 - 3 hours before adding to the salad. The cranberries soaked in the dressing keep well in the fridge for up to 2 days.

Baby Potatoes with Fresh Chopped Dill & Buttermilk Dressing

The fresh chopped dill not only makes this salad attractive but adds flavour and character

Serves 6 - 8

Vegetarian

For the salad:

1200 g (3 lbs) baby new potatoes

For the dressing:

1 x 240 ml tub of whipping cream

2 x 375 ml tub of butter milk

2 - 3 garlic cloves, peeled and crushed

2 - 3 tbsp fresh dill, finely chopped

Salt and pepper

1. Boil the potatoes, drain and allow to cool. Then cut into bite-size pieces.
2. Lightly whip the cream to a mayonnaise consistency.
3. In a large bowl, combine the cream, butter milk, garlic and dill. Then add the potatoes. Season with salt and pepper to taste.

Prepare ahead:

This salad keeps well in the fridge for up to 2 days.

Cantaloupe Melon with Cucumber & Fresh Mint Dressing

I love this salad because it is very fresh and light.

Serves 4 - 6

Vegetarian

1 Cantaloupe melon, peeled and deseeded

1 cucumber, deseeded

6 - 7 tbsp Greek yoghurt

Small handful of fresh chopped mint

Cut the melon and cucumber into bite-size pieces. Then in a large bowl, mix all the ingredients together.

Prepare ahead:
This salad keeps well in the fridge for up to 1 day. Add the fresh chopped mint just before serving.

Waldorf Salad with Pecan Nuts

This effortless, salad goes well with most dishes and keeps well in the fridge for up to 1 day.
Serves 8 - 10
Vegetarian

For the dressing:
150 ml (6 fl oz) Greek yoghurt or light
   crème fraiche
4 tbsp mayonnaise
150 ml (6 fl oz) single cream

Pinch of cinnamon or mixed spice
   (optional)
Salt and pepper

For the salad:
6 Granny Smith apples, unpeeled, cored
   and chopped into small cubes
1 whole celery, washed, trimmed and
   finely chopped

1 celeriac, about 300 g (11 oz) peeled and
   sliced into very fine cubes
50 g (2 oz) pecan nuts, broken into
   small pieces

1. First make the dressing. In a small bowl, mix the yoghurt or light crème fraiche with mayonnaise, cream and cinnamon or mixed spice.
2. In a large bowl, combine the salad ingredients. Then pour the dressing over and mix well. Season with salt and pepper to taste.

Beetroot Salsa

This delicious garlicky salsa is a great accompaniment to mushroom and chestnut risotto or quinoa salad or potato and broccoli frittata - see pages 133, 137, 152.

> TIP:
> * Grating beetroot can easily stain your hands. I always avoid this by wearing rubber gloves.

Serves 4 - 6
Vegetarian

1 x 250 g (10 oz) pack ready cooked and
   peeled beetroot, coarsely grated
2 tbsp mayonnaise
6 - 8 tbsp natural yoghurt
1 - 2 garlic cloves, peeled and crushed

Handful of fresh mint, or rocket finely
   chopped
Dash of lemon juice
Salt and pepper

In a medium bowl, mix all the ingredients together. Taste and adjust the seasoning.

Prepare ahead:
This salsa keeps well in the fridge for up to 2 days.

Cole Slaw for all Seasons with Light Tangy Plum Sauce Dressing

The plum sauce gives a delightful oriental flavour to this colourful salad.
Serves 10 - 12
Vegetarian

1 sweetheart young cabbage, about 600 g (1 lb 5 oz), washed and finely chopped

1 small red cabbage, about 200 g (8 oz), washed and finely chopped

2 large carrots, peeled and grated

1 bunch of spring onions, trimmed and finely chopped

2 oranges peeled and cut into small segments, or 1 can of tangerines drained

2 - 3 tbsp toasted sesame seeds

2 - 3 tbsp plum sauce, to taste

Salt and pepper

In a large bowl, combine all the ingredients together, taste and adjust the seasoning.

Prepare ahead:
This salad keeps well in the fridge for up to 1 day.

Watermelon & Feta Salad

This is a very popular Middle Eastern summer salad. The combination of the sweet crunch of the watermelon with sharp feta cheese adds interest to this simple salad.
Serves 5 - 7
Vegetarian

1 medium water melon, peeled and cut into 2½ cm (1 in) chunks

200 g (7 oz) feta cheese, crumbled

Small handful of fresh chopped mint or shredded basil leaves

50 g (2 oz) walnut pieces

In a large bowl carefully mix the water melon, feta, and herb. Transfer to a large serving platter and scatter the walnuts over the salad.

Prepare ahead:
This salad, without herb and walnuts, keeps well in the fridge for up to 1 day.

Carrot, Apple & Fresh Mint Coleslaw

A beautiful salad, which can accompany most dishes.
Serves 10 - 12

For the salad:

1200 g (2 lbs 10 oz) carrots, peeled and grated

4 Granny Smith apples, unpeeled, cored and finely chopped

6 celery sticks, finely chopped

6 spring onions, trimmed and finely chopped

1 red chilli, deseeded and finely chopped

2 - 3 tbsp fresh mint, finely chopped

For the dressing:

3 tbsp French salad dressing or Basic Vinaigrette - see page 164.

7 tbsp natural Greek yoghurt

3 tbsp mayonnaise

Salt and pepper

1. First make the dressing. In a small bowl, mix together the French dressing, yoghurt and mayonnaise.
2. Place all the salad ingredients in a large bowl and pour the dressing over and mix well. Season with salt and pepper to taste.

VARIATION

Carrot, Chilli & Coconut Salad

Serves 5 - 7

For the dressing mix together:

3 tbsp French salad dressing or Basic Vinaigrette - see page 164.

1 - 2 tbsp mayonnaise

2 - 3 tbsp Greek yoghurt

For the salad:

In a large bowl, combine:

900 g (2 lbs) carrots peeled and grated

2 red peppers deseeded and finely diced

1 green chilli deseeded and finely chopped

3 - 4 spring onions, finely chopped

3 tbsp unsweetened coconut flakes

Salt and pepper

Then pour the dressing over, mix well and season with salt and pepper to taste.

Carrots, Sweet Piquante Peppers, Walnut & Cucumber with Creamy Vinaigrette Dressing

Serves 6 - 7

For the dressing:

Use the same dressing as for the Carrot, Chilli and Coconut Salad.

For the salad:

In a large bowl, combine:

900 g (2 lbs) carrots peeled and grated

1 cucumber deseeded and finely chopped

5 - 6 mild sweet piquante peppers deseeded and finely chopped

75 g (3 oz) walnuts roughly chopped

Then pour the dressing over, mix well and season with salt and pepper to taste.

Carrot with Cinnamon, Lemon & Honey Dressing

Serves 5 - 7

For the dressing:

In a small bowl, mix together:

50 ml (2 fl oz) olive oil

Juice of 2 lemons

½ tsp cinnamon

2 tbsp clear honey

For the salad:

In a large bowl, combine:

900 g (2 lbs) carrots peeled and grated,

75 g (3 oz) washed raisins

75 g (3 oz) toasted almonds

Then add the dressing, mix well and season with salt and pepper to taste.

Prepare ahead:

The dressing and the undressed salad keep well in the fridge for up to 2 days.
Add the dressing to the salad a couple of hours before serving.

Crunchy Coleslaw with Light Orange Dressing

This simple salad tastes superb. Prepare it 1 - 2 days in advance to enhance its flavour.

Serves 5 - 7

Vegetarian

1 sweet heart cabbage about 450 g (1 lb) washed and finely chopped

450 g (1 lb) carrots peeled and grated

200 ml (7 fl oz) fresh orange juice, to taste

4 - 5 tbsp olive oil

Salt and pepper

In a large bowl, mix all the ingredients together and season to taste.

Carrot & Cucumber Salsa

Serves 5 - 7

Vegetarian

½ cucumber, grated

2 large carrots, peeled and grated

1 x 500 g tub natural Greek yoghurt

1 garlic clove, peeled and crushed

1 - 1½ tbsp freshly chopped mint or ½ tsp dried mint

2 tbsp mayonnaise

Small handful of chopped walnuts
    (optional)

Salt and pepper

In a medium bowl, mix together all the ingredients. Season with salt and pepper to taste.

Prepare ahead:
This salsa keeps well in the fridge for up to 1 day.

Cucumber and Tomato Salsa with a Mint & Coriander Dressing

The fresh mint, coriander and lime dressing give this simple salsa an authentic Middle Eastern flavour.

Serves 4 - 6

Vegetarian

For the dressing:

3 tbsp olive oil

1 - 1½ tbsp fresh lime juice

1 garlic clove, peeled and crushed
    (optional)

Salt and pepper

For the salad:

1 large cucumber, deseeded and finely
    chopped

4 medium tomatoes deseeded and finely
    chopped or 15 - 16 cherry tomatoes
    halved or quartered

3 spring onions, trimmed and finely
    chopped

4 radishes, trimmed and finely sliced

2 tbsp chopped fresh mint

1 - 2 tbsp chopped fresh coriander

1. First make the dressing. In a small bowl, whisk together olive oil, lime juice and garlic, if using.
2. In a large bowl, mix all the salad ingredients. Pour the dressing over and gently toss. Season to taste.

Prepare ahead:
This salad undressed keeps well in the fridge for up to 1 day.

Avocado, Blueberry and Feta Cheese Salad with ginger & lime dressing

This exquisite salad also makes a lovely starter.

Serves 5 - 7

Vegetarian

For the dressing:

4 tbsp water

2 tbsp sugar

Juice of 2 limes

2½ cm (1 in) piece of fresh ginger,
    peeled and grated, about 1 - 1½ tsp, to
    taste

125 g (5 oz) fresh or frozen and
defrosted blueberries

Salt and pepper

For the salad:

2 large ripe avocados
Juice of 1 lime
200 g (8 oz) lamb lettuce
About 100 g (4 oz) feta cheese, finely
chopped

125 g (5 oz) fresh or frozen and
defrosted blueberries
Small handful of toasted almond flakes
or pine nuts

1. First make the dressing. In a small saucepan, place the water and sugar. Bring to the boil and simmer over a low heat for 1 - 2 minutes or until the sugar is dissolved. Next add the lime juice, grated ginger and the blueberries. Mix well before removing from the heat. Allow to cool.
2. Then whiz in a blender. Taste and adjust the seasoning.
3. A couple of hours before serving, halve the avocadoes, remove the stones, peel and cut the flesh into bite-size chunks. Then gently toss them in the lime juice to delay browning.
4. Place the lamb lettuce on a serving platter and arrange the avocadoes and feta cheese on top. Drizzle with the dressing and scatter over the blueberries and almond flakes or pine nuts.

Prepare ahead:
This dressing will keep well in the fridge for up to 3 days.

Dressings – The Soul of Salads

Salad dressings give identity to a salad. The right salad dressing makes all the ingredients come to life. Correct proportions are key. Dress your salad with care and with just enough dressing to enhance its flavour.

Basic dressings are made using a loose formula - three parts of oil (any oil you fancy) to one part acid (any vinegar or lemon juice), add salt and pepper plus a small amount of something fiery (mustard, Worcestershire sauce, Tabasco sauce) and an equally small quantity of something sweet (brown sugar or honey).

Extra-virgin olive oil is best for salad dressings but has a strong taste and should be used sparingly. For a lighter dressing, use combination of oils such as olive oil with groundnut oil or sunflower oil.

Note:
One serving equals approximately 2 tablespoons of dressing.

Basic Vinaigrette

This is a good all-rounder for most salads and can be used for glazing fish or chicken.

1 tbsp lemon juice

1 tbsp white wine vinegar 1 tsp Dijon mustard

½ tsp honey (optional)

3 tbsp extra-virgin olive oil

3 tbsp either rapeseed or grape seed oil

Sea salt and black pepper

1. In a clean jar, put the juice, vinegar, mustard and honey and mix with a fork until smoothly combined.
2. Pour in the oil, lightly season, then put the lid on tightly and shake until blended.

This dressing will keep for a couple of weeks in the fridge. Whisk well before serving.

The addition of 1 tbsp of a finely chopped red onion and herbs such as parsley, thyme, chives and tarragon to the vinaigrette will make the dressing more interesting.

Another good dressing for green salads is walnut oil mixed equally with lemon and orange juice and seasoning. This dressing is great with chicken or duck too.

Creamy Dressing

In this dressing, some of the oil is replaced with mayonnaise, single cream, crème fraiche, sour cream or full fat yoghurt. This dressing can be stored in a jar in the fridge for up to 1 week. The mixture may separate as it stands, so whisk well before serving.

Balsamic Vinaigrette Dressing

Balsamic vinaigrette adds extra interest to a salad. It is delicious, quick and easy to prepare.

Serves 5 - 6

Whisk together:

9 tbsp olive oil

3 tbsp balsamic vinegar

1 tsp Dijon mustard

1 garlic clove, peeled and crushed

Season to taste and store as per Basic Vinaigrette.

Creamy Balsamic Dressing

Serves 9 - 10

Place the following in a bowl:

8 tbsp natural full fat Greek

8 tbsp rapeseed or grape seed oil,

3 tbsp balsamic vinegar,

1 tbsp lemon juice

½ tsp Dijon mustard

Whisk together and season to taste. Store as per Creamy Dressing.

Simple Dressings

The simplest dressing, fat-free and virtually calorie-free, is a light sprinkling of balsamic vinegar. You can also mix in Dijon mustard, salt, a pinch of cinnamon, orange juice or red wine vinegar to taste.

With half the fat of traditional vinaigrette, another dressing is light olive oil mixed in equal amounts with balsamic or red wine vinegar and grape or orange juice, again with flavourings such as garlic, mustard, salt, black pepper, sugar, herbs, finely chopped red onion or chilli.

Fat-free, Spicy Dressing for Asian-style Salads

Make the dressing with equal quantities of lime juice, rice wine vinegar and fish sauce mixed with crushed garlic and chopped fresh red chilli and a dash of runny honey.

Japanese Dressing

With its lovely oriental flavour, it seems a million miles from vinaigrette but it is not that different. A dash of it makes a simple green salad more interesting.

Serves 4 - 5

To make the dressing, mix together:

4 tbsp vegetable oil	½ small red onion, peeled and finely chopped
2 tbsp sesame oil	
2 tbsp rice vinegar	1 tsp grated ginger
2 tbsp light soy sauce	1 garlic clove, peeled and crushed

Note:

Rice wine vinegar is sweet and less pungent than grape vinegar and is best used for Japanese-style dressing.

No bake cranberry cheesecake

Puddings with Pizzazz

Puddings are the grand finale of a meal, the memory that guests take away with them. For desserts, I always like to offer a choice so that it makes the meal more of a treat.

This section offers a variety of appetizing puddings to please any taste and any dietary preference.

To make your puddings a huge success, here are a few suggestions.

Chocolate

Use good quality chocolate which makes a big difference to the deliciousness of your pudding. Chocolate with around 60 - 65% cocoa solids is ideal. Anything higher will be too bitter.

To melt chocolate:

Break the chocolate up into small pieces and place them into a heat-proof bowl and set over a small saucepan of warm water. Heat the water until it just begins to boil. Remove the saucepan from the heat and allow the chocolate to melt slowly. Stir every now and then until the chocolate is melted and smooth.

Pastry

I found following these few simple rules ensures the pastry is crisp and fully cooked.

To roll out the pastry:

1. Cut two pieces of cling film larger than the size of your pie dish or flan tin.
2. Place the pastry between the two sheets of cling film. Using a rolling pin, gently roll out the pastry until it is 3 - 4 mm thick. If you want to roll out your pastry to a round shape, you need to give the pastry a quarter-turn after each rolling. Make sure it is even in thickness and is large enough to line the base and sides of the tin.

Transferring pastry to a tin:

1. Remove the top layer of cling film and slide your hands under the bottom layer of the cling film. Turn over the pastry and carefully place it evenly into the tart tin so that the cling film is now on top.
2. Gently press the pastry with the cling film still attached into the edges and the corners of the tin so that no air is trapped underneath. Ease back any overlapping bits into the tin, as the stretched pastry will shrink in the oven.
3. Remove the cling film.
4. Trim off any excess pastry from the outside. Prick the pastry base gently all over with a fork to release any trapped air as this prevents it rising during baking.
5. Then chill in the fridge for 20 - 30 minutes.

Baking Blind:

Lightly brush the pastry base with some beaten egg, as this helps to keep the pastry crisp before the filling goes in. Place the tin in the pre-heated oven and bake as instructed in the recipe. Check the pastry after 6 - 8 minutes and, if it is puffing up, gently press it down and prick again.

To remove the tart or pie from a flan tin with a removable base:

1. Let the tart cool.
2. Place it on an upside down bowl and carefully push the ring down and off the pastry.
3. Transfer the tart with the base on to a serving platter and gently slide the tart off the base.

Eggs:

Never use an egg with a cracked shell because it is easy for bacteria to get in. To test the age of an egg, place it in a bowl of cool water. Fresh eggs will sink, while older eggs float to the surface. Never use old eggs. Eggs keep in the fridge for about three weeks. Store them in the lowest part of the refrigerator and away from foods with strong smells, as their shells are porous and can easily absorb flavours. Always bring eggs to room temperature before using. This helps to avoid curdling in cake recipes and cracking when boiled.

Gelatine:

Instead of conventional gelatine, you may use agar-agar (vegetable gelatine). 3½ gelatine leaves is equal to 1 tablespoon powdered gelatine. The best way to dissolve the powdered gelatine is to sprinkle into a small heat-proof bowl containing 2 - 3 tablespoons of water. Stir and leave to soften for about 5 minutes. Then place the bowl over a small pan of barely simmering water, stirring every now and then until the gelatine is completely dissolved and turned transparent. Do not allow the liquid to boil.

Freezing cheesecake:

Fully wrap the un-decorated cheesecake in waxed paper, then place it in a freezer bag and freeze for up to 1 month.

To use:

Thaw the cheesecake overnight in the fridge and decorate before serving.

TIPS:

- To retrieve cream which has been over-whipped, just add a drop of milk.
- Add a pinch of salt to your cake batter. It enhances the flavour of other ingredients and brings out the sweetness.

Fresh Fruit with Passion Fruit Cream & Crème De Cassis

This very simple dessert looks and tastes stunning.

Serves 12 - 15

300 ml (11 fl oz) double cream

1½ - 2 tbsp caster sugar to taste

4 - 5 tbsp Crème De Cassis

4 - 5 ripe passion fruits (see Tip)

A selection of fresh fruit such as figs, strawberries, red grapes, wedges of red apples and mango cubes.

1. Whip the cream with the sugar until thick.
2. Cut the passion fruits in half, scoop out all the pulp and seeds and add them to the cream. Then stir in the Crème De Cassis and whip until well mixed. Serve as a dip for the fruit.

VARIATIONS

Passion Fruit Cream with Elderflower Cordial

Make the recipe in the same way. Just replace the Crème De Cassis with 3 - 4 tbsp of elderflower cordial and add an extra 1 - 2 tbsp of sugar to the cream.

Passion Fruit Cream

Make the recipe in the same way. Just leave out the Crème De Cassis.

Prepare ahead:
Flavoured creams keep well in the fridge for up to 1 - 2 days.

TIP:

• Dark wrinkled passion fruits have the sweetest and most perfumed juice.

Cranachan

Prepare this lovely Scottish dessert 1 - 2 days in advance to enhance its flavour. It looks pretty in a glass serving dish.

Serves 9 - 11

150 g (6 oz) rolled oats

600 ml (1 pin) double cream

6 - 7 tbsp of clear runny honey (to taste)

2½ cm (1 in) piece of fresh ginger,
   peeled and grated, about 1 tsp, to taste

500 g (1 lb 2 oz) fresh raspberries
  (safe a few of the best for decoration
  of the top)

1. Heat a non-stick frying pan, spread the oats in the pan and toast over a medium-low heat until lightly brown. To prevent the oats from burning, stir continuously.
2. Remove from the heat and cool.
3. In a large bowl mix the cream, oatmeal, honey and ginger.
4. Spread 1/3 of the oatmeal mixture on the base of a serving dish. Put 1/3 of the raspberries on, then lay another 1/3 oatmeal cream, topped with 1/3 raspberries, and finally another 1/3 oatmeal topped with the rest of the raspberries. In this way, the raspberries will not squash and stay whole.

VARIATIONS

Make the recipe in the same way but just use one of the following:

Cranachan with Whisky

Replace the ginger with 1 - 2 tbsp of Whisky, Drambuie or Rum.

Cranachan with Orange Marmalade

For a zesty flavour replace 3 tbsp of honey, with 3 - 4 tbsp of orange marmalade, to taste.

Dates stuffed with Marzipan & drizzled with Dark Chocolate

These bite-sized sweet nibbles, with their lovely dark chocolate crust, look stunning on a large platter surrounded with sweet juicy strawberries. They can be made quickly and easily for any number of people.

Makes 24

About 75 g (3 oz) ground almonds	½ tsp grated zest of orange or a dash of vanilla essence
About 37 g (1½ oz) caster sugar	
2 tbsp water	24 soft dates, stoned

For the chocolate sauce:

50 g (2 oz) good quality plain chocolate (60 - 65% cocoa solids)	2 tbsp water

1. In a small bowl, mix the ground almond, sugar, water and orange zest or vanilla essence until it forms a paste. Add a drop more water if necessary.
2. With a sharp knife, slit the side of dates and stuff each with a teaspoon of almond paste.
3. Place the chocolate with the water in a small bowl set over a pan of hot water. Stir occasionally until the chocolate is melted. Remove from the heat. Then drizzle over the dates.

Prepare ahead:

The dates prepared to the end of step 2 keep well in a cool place for up to 2 days.

To use:

Drizzle with the melted chocolate 3 - 4 hours before serving.

Mango, Orange & Chocolate with Pistachio

This light and tasty dessert with no eggs or wheat pleases any taste. It is very easy to prepare for any number of people and keeps well in the fridge for up to 2 days.

Serves 6 - 7

    200 g (8 oz) good quality plain chocolate (60 – 65 % cocoa solids), chopped

3 tbsp orange juice

Grated zest of 1 small orange

2 large ripe mangoes

1 x 250 g tub of light mascarpone

About 75 g (3 oz) chopped pistachio save 2 tbsp to decorate the top-see note 2

To decorate:

Mango cubes and chopped pistachio or toasted almond flakes

1. Place the chocolate with the orange juice and orange zest in a small bowl set over a pan of hot water. Stir occasionally until the chocolate is melted. Then remove from the heat and set aside to cool.
2. Peel and grate 1½ mangoes, and chop the rest of the flesh into small cubes.
3. In a large bowl, combine the grated mango, mascarpone, chocolate mixture, pistachio or almond flakes and any mango juice on your cutting board
4. Transfer to a serving dish, decorate with the mango cubes and sprinkle with the chopped pistachio or almond flakes.

Serve with a plate of Crispy Biscuit Curls

Notes:

1. You may serve this dessert in individual wine or champagne glasses.
2. The pistachio could be replaced with lightly toasted almond flakes.

Dark Chocolate & Coffee Refrigerator Cake

If you like coffee, you will love this dessert. It requires no baking. Prepare it 1 - 2 days in advance to enhance its flavour.

Serves 7 - 8

100 g (4 oz) good quality plain chocolate (60 - 65% cocoa solids), chopped plus extra, about 25 g (1 oz) for decoration

2 tbsp water

300 ml (11 fl oz) whipping cream

4 teaspoons instant coffee powder

180 ml (7 fl oz) warm water

100 g (4 oz) sugar

30 sponge finger biscuits

To decorate:

Roughly grated dark chocolate

1. Place the chocolate with the 2 tbsp of water in a small bowl set over a pan of hot water. Stir occasionally until the chocolate is melted. Remove from the heat and set aside to cool.
2. Whip the cream until thick, and then fold in the cool, melted chocolate.
3. Place the coffee, water and sugar in a small pot over a low heat. Stir until the sugar is dissolved
4. Divide the sponge fingers into two groups of 15. Dip one sponge finger at a time in the warm coffee but do not leave it for too long as it may fall apart. Place it on a serving dish. Once you have a neat row of 15 moist sponge fingers, spread half of the chocolate cream over them. Follow this with another layer of sponge fingers dipped again in the warm coffee. Then spread the remaining chocolate cream over the top and sides of the cake.
5. Sprinkle with the grated chocolate and chill in the fridge for several hours or overnight.

VARIATION

Dark Chocolate & Rum Refrigerator Cake

Replace the coffee with rum syrup.

For the rum syrup:

1. Place the 100 g (4 oz) sugar with 110 ml (4 fl oz) of warm water in a small pan.
2. Dissolve the sugar over a low heat. Remove from the heat and add 4 tablespoons of rum. Allow to cool slightly then follow the recipe above.

No Bake Cranberry Cheesecake

Years ago I had this festive light cheesecake at a Thanksgiving party in my sister in-law's house in Texas. It was so scrumptious that it has stayed on my entertaining menu since then.

Serves 6 - 8 (to serve 10 - 12, see recipe below)

For the topping:

60 g (2½ oz) caster sugar

2 tbsp water

200 g (8 oz) fresh or frozen and
defrosted cranberries

Grated zest of one lemon

1 tbsp lemon juice

For the base:

90 g (3½ oz) unsalted butter, diced

175 g (7 oz) digestive biscuits

1 tsp almond essence

For the cheesecake:

3 gelatine leaves soaked in 300 ml (½
pint) of cold water for 10 minutes
then drained

2 tbsp lemon juice (remember you get
some tartness from cranberries too)

250 ml (9 fl oz) double cream

200 g (8 oz) cream cheese

200 g (8 oz) light condensed milk

Grated zest of one lemon

½ tsp almond essence

To decorate:

A handful of chopped pistachio

Use a lightly greased 21 - 22 cm (8½ in) shallow pie dish or flan tin with a removable base.

1. First make the topping. In a medium pan, dissolve the sugar in the water over a low heat. Add the cranberries, lemon zest and lemon juice and simmer gently for 4 - 5 minutes. Stir occasionally until the cranberries start to burst (but not mushy) and the mixture is slightly thickened. Remove from the heat and cool.

2. Place the biscuits into a food processor and whiz until you have really fine crumbs. Alternatively, put the biscuits in a plastic bag and crush to crumbs with a rolling pin.

3. Melt the butter in a pan. Stir in the crushed biscuits and almond essence. Mix well.

4. Spread the biscuit mixture around the base of the pie dish or flan tin, then use the back of a spoon to flatten it into the base and up the sides of the tin. To make sure the mixture gets right to the edges, press it down with your fingertips.

5. Next place the tin on a flat platter or a baking sheet and chill in the fridge for 1 - 2 hours or until firm.

6. Place the gelatine leaves with 2 tablespoons of lemon juice in a small bowl set over a pan of hot water. Stir for 1 - 2 minutes or until the gelatine is dissolved. Then remove from the heat and set aside to cool slightly.

7. Meanwhile, in a large bowl, whip the cream until thick. Fold in the cream cheese, condensed milk, lemon zest and almond essence.

8. Then carefully add the gelatine mixture and mix thoroughly.

9. Spread half of the cheese mixture over the biscuit case then scatter over with about ½ of cranberries. Cover the cranberries with the remaining mixture. Smooth the surface. Cover and chill in the fridge for 4 - 5 hours or until set.

10. If have used a flan tin, remove the cheese cake from the tin (you may leave the base of the tin still attached) and carefully transfer it to a serving platter.

11. Arrange the rest of the cranberries on top of the cheesecake and sprinkle with the chopped pistachios.

Serves 10 - 12

For the topping:

Double the amount of cranberries, sugar and water and lemon zest

For the base:

125 g (5 oz) unsalted butter, diced
250 g (10 oz) digestive biscuits, crushed
1½ tsp almond essence

For the cheesecake:

5 gelatine leaves soaked in 300 ml (½ pint) of cold water for 10 minutes, then drained

4 tbsp lemon juice (remember you get
Some tartness from cranberries too)

450 ml (16 fl oz) double cream
300 g (11 oz) cream cheese
405 g tin of light condensed milk
Grated zest of 2 lemons
1 - 1½ tsp almond essence

Use a lightly greased 24 cm (9½ in) shallow pie dish or flan tin with a removable base. Then make the recipe in the same way.

Prepare ahead:

Cranberries prepared to the end of step 1 keep well in the fridge for up to 1 week and in the freezer for up to 1 month. Cheesecake keeps well in the fridge for up to 2 days.

To freeze:

You may also freeze this cheesecake - see page 169.

VARIATION

No Bake Cheesecake with fresh strawberries

Convert it to a lovely summer pudding by replacing the cranberries with about 450 g (1 lb) finely sliced fresh strawberries

Prepare the cheesecake from steps 2 - 7. For a more pronounced flavour, add extra grated zest of ½ lemon and 1 tbsp lemon juice to the cheesecake mixture. At step 8, instead of cranberries, spoon half of the strawberries over the cheese mixture, and then complete the recipe.

Note:

You may use agar-agar, a vegetable gelatine or powdered gelatine - see page 169.

Exquisite Petits Fours

These delicious little chocolates can be served as dessert canapé or with a cup of hot coffee at the end of a meal. With just a few ingredients, they are easy to make at any time and keep well in the fridge for 3 - 4 days. To store, please see Tip further on in this section.

Petits fours also make a lovely gift, by arranging a few in a pretty little box tied with ribbon.

Dark Chocolate Truffle Cakes

Makes 32 - 34 marble-size truffles

125 g (5 oz) trifle sponge cakes

5 tbsp apricot jam, to taste

2 tbsp hot water

125 g (5 oz) ground almond

For the chocolate icing:

100 g (4 oz) good quality plain chocolate
(60 - 65% cocoa solids), chopped

6 tbsp water

To decorate:

Use approx. 50 g (2 oz) of your preferred ingredients such as unsweetened coconut flakes or finely chopped hazelnuts, pistachios, almond flakes or pecan nuts

1. Place the trifle cakes into a food processor and whiz until you have got really fine crumbs. Alternatively, finely grate the trifle cakes, using a cheese grater.

2. In a small saucepan, heat the apricot jam with the water.

3. Place the crumbs, ground almond and hot apricot in a medium bowl and mix well. Then bring the mixture together with your hands to form a smooth ball of dough.

4. Lightly coat your hands in flavourless oil, such as sunflower and shape the mixture into about 2½ cm (1 in) marble-size balls. Place them on a tray lined with waxed paper and chill for 20 - 30 minutes or until cold and firm.

5. Meanwhile sprinkle a small handful of your preferred finish on a flat plate.

6. Line a large tray with waxed paper.

7. Place the chocolate and water in a small bowl set over a pan of hot water. Stir occasionally until the chocolate is melted.

8. Dip the truffle balls one at a time into the warm chocolate. Lift out with a fork, drain and then gently roll round in the nuts until evenly coated. Place the truffles on the prepared tray.

9. Refrigerate for 2 - 3 hours or until set firm.

Cardamom Chocolate Discs with Cranberries and Pistachio

These elegant little chocolates are versatile. You can vary their flavour and the toppings. They also keep well in freezer for up to 1 month if stored in an air tight container. When ready to use, leave the chocolate discs to defrost at cool room temperature for 1 - 2 hours.

Makes about 30 - 35 chocolate discs

75 g (3 oz) good quality plain chocolate (60 - 65% cocoa solids), chopped

25 g (1 oz) white chocolate, chopped

2 tbsp double cream

7 cardamom pods, lightly crushed and husk removed - see page 66

50 g (2 oz) dried cranberries

25 g (1 oz) chopped pistachio nuts

1. Place the chocolates, cream and crushed cardamom seeds in a small bowl set over a pan of hot water. Stir occasionally until the chocolate is melted.

2. Meanwhile line a large tray with waxed paper.

3. Carefully drop teaspoonfuls of the melted chocolate on the tray, making sure that you leave a gap of 2 cm (½ in) between the discs as they will spread out slightly.

4. While the chocolate is still liquid, top with a couple of cranberries and a sprinkle of pistachio.

5. Refrigerate the chocolates for 2 - 3 hours or until they set firm before lifting off the paper.

Variations

Mint Chocolate Discs with Pistachio

Make the recipe in the same way. Replace the cardamom with ½ teaspoon of peppermint extract or slightly more to taste. Leave out the cranberries. Sprinkle the chocolate discs with the chopped pistachio nuts.

Vary the flavouring: Use other delicious flavourings such as vanilla extract, or hazelnut, raspberry or orange liqueurs.

Chocolate Discs with Crystallized Ginger & Almond Flakes

Make the recipe in the same way. Replace the cardamom with 30 g (1½ oz) finely chopped crystallized ginger. Sprinkle the chocolate discs with the almond flakes.
Vary the toppings: Dried cherries, raisins, roughly chopped hazelnuts, pecan nuts or walnuts also make lovely toppings.

TIP:

- To store the petits fours, place the Chocolate Truffle Cakes or Chocolate Discs in an air-tight container. Cover them with a piece of waxed paper before securing the lid as they might sweat. Then store in the fridge for 3 - 4 days.

Apple Tart

This delicious tart tastes even better if it is prepared 1 - 2 days in advance to allow the flavours to mingle.
You may leave out the flaked almonds, if you wish. Sprinkling the tart the almonds enhances flavour and attraction.

Serves 5 - 6 (To serve 8 - 10, see recipe below)

350 g (13 oz) ready-made dessert pastry	1 egg yolk beaten
100 g (4 oz) lightly salted butter, diced	2 medium size cooking apples, approx.
100 g (4 oz) caster sugar	450 g (1 lb) peeled, cored and coarsely
1 tsp vanilla essence	grated
Grated zest of small lemon, about ½ tsp	50 g (2 oz) flaked almonds
1 large egg beaten	

Use a lightly greased 21 - 22 cm (8½ in) shallow pie dish or flan tin with a removable base.

1. Line the pie dish or flan tin with the pastry and prick gently all over the base with a fork to release any trapped air. Then chill in the fridge for 20 - 30 minutes.
2. Pre-heat oven to 190 °C / 380 °F / Gas mark 5.
3. Place the pastry in the pre-heated oven and bake for 10 - 12 minutes or until the pastry feels dry in the base.
4. Meanwhile melt the butter in a saucepan, draw off the heat and stir in the sugar. Let it cool.
5. Stir into the butter mixture the vanilla essence, lemon zest, eggs, egg yolk and apples. Mix well. Then spoon the apple mixture into the pastry case and smooth the surface. Sprinkle with flaked almonds.

6. Bake the tart for 25 - 30 minutes or until it is golden and a skewer or cocktail stick inserted into the middle comes out clean. Check after 15 - 20 minutes if the almonds have started to brown. Loosely cover the tart with a piece of tin foil, greaseproof paper or baking parchment. The filling may puff but falls back quickly once you bring it out of the oven. Allow to cool.

7. If you have used a flan tin, remove the tart from the tin (with the base of the tin still attached) and carefully transfer it to a serving platter.

8. Serve with a dollop of cream or a scoop of ice cream.

To serve 8 - 10

1 x 375 g pack dessert pastry

135 g (5½ oz) lightly salted butter, diced

135 g (5½ oz) caster sugar

1½ tsp vanilla essence

Grated zest of 1 small lemon,
   about 1 tsp

2 large eggs beaten

1 egg yolk beaten

4 cooking apples about 650 g, (1 lb 7 oz)
   peeled, cored and coarsely grated

60 g (2½ oz) flaked almonds

Use a 24 cm (9½ in) lightly greased shallow pie dish or flan tin with a removable base.

Follow the instructions as in the above recipe. Bake the tart for 35 - 40 minutes or until it is golden. Check after 15 - 20 minutes if the almonds have started to brown. Place a piece of tin foil, greaseproof paper or baking parchment loosely over the tart.

TIP:

- Store the tart in a cool place.

Pecan Pie

This gorgeous sticky pie with chunks of pecans and vanilla flavour attracts the eyes on any autumn or Christmas buffet. With all its temptations, it demands little preparation and keeps well in a cool place for up to 2 - 3 days.

Serves 6 - 7 (To serve 8 - 10, see recipe below)

300 g (12 oz) pre-rolled short crust
   pastry from a pack

110 g (4½ oz) pecan halves

50 g (2 oz) softened butter

100 g (4 oz) light brown sugar

200 g (8 oz) golden syrup

3 large eggs lightly beaten

1½ tsp plain flour

2 tsp vanilla

Grated zest of 1small lemon,
   about ½ teaspoon

1. Use a 21 - 22 cm (8½ in) lightly greased shallow pie dish or flan tin with a removable base.

2. Line the pie dish or flan tin with the pastry and prick gently all over the base with a fork to release any trapped air. Then chill in the fridge for 20 - 30 minutes.

3. Pre-heat oven to 190 °C / 380 °F / Gas mark 5.

4. Place the pastry in the pre-heated oven and bake for 10 - 12 minutes or until the pastry feels dry in the base. Remove from the oven and place the pecan nuts evenly over the pastry case. Set aside.

5. Reduce the heat to 150 °C / 300 °F / Gas mark 2.

6. Meanwhile lightly whisk together the butter and sugar. Add the syrup, eggs, flour, vanilla essence and lemon zest. Mix thoroughly.

7. Pour the mixture over the pecan nuts and smooth the surface.

8. Bake the pie for 50 - 55 minutes or until it is lightly golden and a skewer or cocktail stick inserted into the middle comes out clean. The filling will puff but falls back quickly once you bring it out of the oven. Allow to cool.

9. If have used a flan tin, remove the pie from the tin (with the base of the tin still attached) and carefully transfer to a serving platter.

To serve 8 - 10

1 x 375 g pack of pre-rolled short crust
  pastry
About 140 g (5½ oz) pecan nuts
  (halves)
75 g (3 oz) butter at room temperature
150 g (6 oz) light brown sugar

250 g (10 oz) golden syrup
4 large eggs, lightly beaten
1 tbsp plain flour
3 tsp vanilla essence
Grated zest of 1 medium lemon,
  about 1 tsp

Use a 24 cm (9½ in) lightly greased shallow pie dish or flan tin with a removable base.
Follow the instructions as in the above recipe. Bake the pie for 50 - 55 minutes or until lightly golden and a skewer or cocktail stick inserted into the middle comes out clean.

Four Seasons Crumble

In this simple, delicious yet economical pudding, the sweetness of pears counteracts the sharpness of the summer fruits. The fruit crumble tastes good if served at room temperature too. Serve with ice cream, single cream or warm custard.
Here are two of my favourite recipes.

Oat & Cinnamon Crumble

Serves 6 - 8

For the crumble:

200 g (8 oz) porridge oats
1½ tsp ground cinnamon
110 g (4½ oz) soft dark brown sugar

110 g (4½ oz) butter at room
  temperature

For the fruit:

  1 x 500 g pack of frozen summer fruits, defrosted overnight in the fridge - see Note 1

  3 medium Granny Smith apples, peeled, cored and finely chopped

  3 medium ripe conference pears, peeled, cored and finely chopped

Use a medium size oven proof dish, about 27 x 27 cm. (6½ x 6½ in)

1. Place all the ingredients for the crumble in a large bowl and rub together, using your fingertips, until it looks crumbly.
2. Pre-heat the oven to 190 °C / 380 °F / Gas mark 5.
3. Place all the fruit in the oven proof dish and mix well.
4. Sprinkle the crumble mixture over the fruit, and smooth the surface - do not press it down.
5. Cook the crumble in the oven for about 20 minutes or until the top is lightly golden brown.

VARIATION

Ginger Crumble

A gentle hint of fresh ginger in the fruit adds warmth to this pudding.

Make the recipe in the same way. Just peel and grate 2½ cm (1 in) piece of fresh ginger, about 2 tsps, and add to the fruit mixture in step 3.

Note:

Frozen summer fruits are very economical. A pack usually contains strawberries, blackberries, raspberries, blackcurrants and redcurrants.

You may replace Conference pears with other pears such as Rocha or Packham. No need to peel them.

Persian Almond Macaroons

These tiny elegant macaroons are a tempting sweet for all seasons and can be served in many ways.

You may top the macaroons with whipped cream or chocolate cream one day in advance, loosely cover and store in the fridge. Decorate with berries before serving.

Makes about 30

  2 medium eggs

  130 g (5 oz) caster sugar

½ teaspoon almond essence

Grated zest of 1 lemon

1 - 1½ tsp lemon juice, to taste

160 g (6 oz) ground almonds

¼ tsp baking powder

For the topping:

200 ml (7 fl oz) double cream, whipped

To decorate:

A handful of strawberries washed, hulled and sliced and toasted almond flakes.

1. Pre-heat the oven to 180 °C / 350 °F / Gas mark 4.
2. Whisk the eggs and sugar until thick and pale yellow, about 3 - 4 minutes. Add in the almond essence, lemon zest, lemon juice, and then gently fold in the ground almond and baking powder.
3. Cover a baking tray with baking parchment (see Tip below). Spoon teaspoonfuls of the mixture on to the tray. The macaroons will spread a little while baking, so do leave a gap of 1½ cm (½ in) between them.
4. Bake them in the oven for 10 - 12 minutes or until lightly golden.
5. Remove from the oven and let them cool on the baking parchment for about 10 minutes. Then gently slide a flat knife underneath each macaroon and place them on a wire rack.
6. When ready to serve, top with a dollop of whipped cream, a slice of strawberry and couple of almond flakes.

TIP:

- To stop macaroons sticking to the baking parchment, before spooning on the mixture, dip your fingers in water and swiftly run them over the parchment to make it slightly damp.

VARIATION

Almond Macaroons with Chocolate cream

Make the macaroons in the same way. Replace the cream with chocolate cream.

For the chocolate cream:

50 g (2 oz) good quality plain chocolate (60 - 65% cocoa solids), chopped

1 tbsp water

150 ml (6 fl oz) double cream

To decorate:

A small handful of red berries

1. Place the chocolate with the water in a small bowl set over a pan of hot water. Stir occasionally until the chocolate is melted. Remove from heat and set aside to cool.
2. In a large bowl, whip the cream until thick. Fold in the cool melted chocolate.

Prepare ahead:

The chocolate cream could be prepared 4 - 5 hours in advance and kept in a cool place.

The macaroons stored in an airtight container keep well in the fridge for up to 4 days and in the freezer for up to 1 month. Cover the macaroons with a piece of waxed paper before securing the lid as they might sweat.

To freeze:

Macaroons follow the same instruction as for blinis.

To use:

Frozen macaroons take about 2 - 3 hours to thaw at room temperature or overnight in the fridge.

Blueberry and Strawberry Tart with Vanilla Yoghurt

This light tart complements a rich meal. I first tasted this lovely tart at a Swedish friend's dinner party and since then it is of my favourites.

Serves 7 - 9

1 x 375 g pack of dessert pastry
2 large egg yolks
110 g (4½ oz) caster sugar
120 ml (5 fl oz) milk
Grated zest of 1 lemon
1 tsp vanilla essence

3 gelatine leaves soaked in 300 ml (½ pint) of cold water for 10 minutes, then drained
1 x 500 g tub of natural Greek yoghurt
150 g (6 oz) strawberries, washed, hulled and sliced, plus extra to decorate
150 g (6 oz) blue berries, plus extra to decorate

To decorate:

A handful of chopped unsalted pistachios (optional)

Use a 23 - 24 cm (9 - 9½ in) lightly greased shallow pie dish or flan tin with a removable base.

1. Line the pie dish or flan tin with the pastry and prick gently all over the base with a fork to release any trapped air.
2. Chill in the fridge for 20 - 30 minutes.
3. Pre-heated oven to 190 °C / 380 °F / Gas mark 5.
4. Place the pastry in the pre-heated oven and bake for 15 - 18 minutes or until lightly golden brown. Remove from the oven and cool.
5. In a large bowl, whisk together the egg yolks and sugar until pale. Heat the milk and then pour slowly into the egg mixture. Next transfer the mixture into a large saucepan and

cook over a low heat, stirring continuously until the mixture thickens to the same consistency as custard.

6. Add the lemon zest, vanilla essence and gelatine and stir over a very low heat until the gelatine is dissolved. Making sure it does not come to the boil. Remove and set aside to cool. Stir a few times to prevent a skin forming.

7. When the custard is cool, but not set, fold in the yoghurt.

8. Scatter the strawberries and blueberries evenly over the pastry case. Pour the yoghurt mixture over the fruit. Cover and chill for about 3 hours or until set.

9. If you have used a flan tin, remove the tart from the tin (with the base of the tin still attached) and carefully transfer to a serving platter.

10. Decorate with the berries and chopped pistachio, if using.

Prepare ahead:

The tart keeps well in the fridge for up to 2 days.

Note:

You may use agar-agar, a vegetable gelatine, or powdered gelatine —see page 169.

You can avoid all eggs and still make an excellent cake or tart. Here are my two favourite recipes.

Chocolate, Almond and Pear Tart with No Eggs

This moist tart is made with no eggs or butter. The small chunks of dark chocolate add interest to this lovely tart and the fresh orange juice and orange zest give it a fresh zesty taste. Serve with a dollop of single cream.

Serves 6 (to serve 9 - 10, see recipe below)

50 g (2 oz) self-raising flour

1 tsp baking powder

1 tbsp cocoa

90 g (3½ oz) soft dark brown sugar

75 g (3 oz) ground almond

¼ teaspoon salt

2½ tbsp sunflower oil

100 ml (4 fl oz) soya milk

1 tbsp orange juice

Grated zest of one small orange

50 g (2 oz) good quality plain chocolate
   (60 - 65% cocoa solids), chopped

1 medium crispy conference pear,

about 150 g (6 oz) peeled and thinly
   sliced

To decorate:

Juicy red berries

Use an 18 cm (7 in) spring-release cake tin, lightly greased and lined with baking parchment

1. Pre-heat the oven 180 °C / 350 °F / Gas mark 4.
2. In a large bowl, sift the flour, baking powder and cocoa. Add the brown sugar, ground almond and salt and mix well.
3. Make a well in the centre of the dry ingredients and stir in the oil, soya milk, orange juice and orange zest. Whisk until thoroughly combined. Add the chocolate pieces.
4. Spoon the mixture into the prepared tin and arrange the pear slices neatly on top.
5. Bake for 35 - 40 minutes or until the tart is done and a skewer or cocktail stick inserted into the middle comes out clean.
6. Remove from the oven and allow to cool in the tin for 15 - 20 minutes (see Note below).
7. Cover the tart with a wire rack and carefully turn it upside down. Remove the tin, carefully peel off the greaseproof paper and leave the tart to cool completely.
8. Next gently turn over the tart back on to a serving plate and cover until ready to serve. Decorate with berries before taking to the table.

To serve 9 - 10

1. Lightly grease and line a 22 cm (8½ in) spring-release cake tin with baking parchment.
2. Double the quantity of ingredients used in the above recipe.
3. Then follow the instructions from step 1.
4. Bake the tart for 35 - 40 minutes or until it is done.

TIP:
- Using milk chocolate or over-ripe pear would make the tart too sweet.

Note:

If the tart stays in the tin for too long it becomes soggy.

Prepare ahead:

This tart keeps well in the fridge for up to 2 days.

Light Coconut & Fruit Cake with No Eggs

This cake with its light crumbly texture tastes even more flavourful if it is prepared 1 - 2 days in advance. You may serve it with single cream, although it is delicious on its own.

Serves 7 - 9

175 g (7 oz) plain flour	1½ tsp cinnamon
2 tsp baking powder	125 g (5 oz) unsweetened coconut flakes

100 g (4 oz) currants

Pinch of salt

1 x 405 g tin light condensed milk

250 g (10 oz) melted butter or soya margarine

100 ml (4 fl oz) fresh orange juice

Grated zest of 1 orange

Grated zest of 2 large lemons

1 tbsp lemon juice

Use a 24 cm (9½ in) spring-release cake tin lightly greased and lined with baking parchment.

1. Pre-heat oven to 170 °C / 325 °F / Gas mark 3.

2. In a large bowl, sift together the flour, baking powder and cinnamon. Then add the coconuts, currants and a pinch of salt and make a well in the centre of dry ingredients. Stir in the condensed milk, melted butter or soya margarine, orange juice, orange zest, lemon zest and lemon juice. Mix well. If the mixture is too dry, just add a little more orange juice (about 1 tbsp).

3. Pour the mixture into the prepared cake tin, smooth the surface and make a tiny dip in the centre which helps it to rise evenly. Bake for 35 - 40 minutes or until the cake is golden and a skewer or cocktail stick inserted into the middle comes out clean.

4. Remove the cake from the oven. Allow to cool in the tin for about 20 minutes.

5. Then cover the cake with a wire rack and carefully turn it upside down. Remove the tin, carefully peel off the greaseproof paper and leave the cake to cool completely.

6. Next gently turn over the cake back on to a serving plate and cover until ready to serve.

Light Bites

When entertaining friends in the afternoon or for a drink in the evening, the small bites you offer should be light and interesting. And with all menus, if you wish, you can serve a light hot or cold soup in small cups - see Scrumptious Soups. Here are few suggestions for light bites:

❧❦❧

- ❧ Mini oat cakes with smoked salmon and lumpfish caviar - see page 78
- ❧ Oven-roasted red pepper, red onion and feta cheese with bread sticks - see page 72
- ❧ Guacamole with crudities - see page 69

❧❦❧

- ❧ Oven-baked honey and chilli sausages - see page 90
- ❧ Boursin cheese puffs with sesame and poppy seeds - see pages 83
- ❧ Mini tomatoes sandwiches with mozzarella and basil - see pages 80
- ❧ Smoked rainbow trout with chives on pumpernickel - see pages 79

❧❦❧

- ❧ Curried parsnip chips with a bowl of sour cream or natural Greek yoghurt - see page 75
- ❧ Hummus with roasted pepper - see page 73
- ❧ Roasted sesame pitta wedges - see page 75
- ❧ Platter of crudities

❧❦❧

- ❧ Rosemary prawns and Parma ham skewers - see page 105
- ❧ Persian style mint yoghurt - see page 71
- ❧ Platter of crudities
- ❧ Aduki beans hummus - see page 72
- ❧ Bread sticks or rosemary and garlic crostini - see page 74

❧❦❧

Along with my light bites, I usually like to offer one or two of the following sweet platters:

- ❧ Dates stuffed with marzipan and drizzled with dark chocolate - see page 171
- ❧ Persian almond macaroons - see page 181
- ❧ Petits fours - see page 176
- ❧ Pecan pie - see 179
- ❧ Fresh fruit with passion fruit cream and crème de cassis - see 170

See Puddings with Pizzazz for further ideas.

Casual Lunches and Late Supper Parties

One of my favourite ways to entertain is getting together with friends for a casual meal. It is fairly easy to organize tasty meals that look smart but are simple to cook, whether the occasion is just catching up, playing card games, a book club meeting or after a theatre or concert.

For a casual get together, very often just two courses are sufficient. With a little thought and careful planning, you can create imaginative meals that can be prepared with the minimum of fuss, be economical and yet delicious. Here are few suggestions:

ॐ

- ॐ Persian mint style yoghurt –with crudities - see page 71
- ॐ Oven baked salmon with smoked paprika, coriander and lime juice - see page 108
- ॐ Roasted sweet potato wedges - see page 150
- ॐ No-bake cranberry cheese cake - see page 173

ॐ

- ॐ Cajun seafood casserole - see page 106
- ॐ French beans and petite pois with a tarragon dressing - see page 151
- ॐ Apple tart - see page 178

ॐ

- ॐ Mixed green salad
- ॐ Oven-baked mushroom and chestnut risotto - see page 133
- ॐ Beetroot salsa - see page 159
- ॐ Fresh fruit platter with passion fruit cream - sees page 170

ॐ

- ॐ Broccoli and potato frittata - see page 152
- ॐ Waldorf salad with pecan nuts - see page 159
- ॐ Carrot and cumber salsa - see page 162
- ॐ Dark chocolate and coffee refrigerator cake – see page 173

ॐ

- ॐ Parmesan and sage meatballs with chorizo sauce - see page 129
- ॐ Oven-roasted baby potatoes - see page 77
- ॐ Carrot, apple and fresh mint coleslaw - see page 160
- ॐ Cranachan –see page 170

Small Dinner Parties
(for 2 - 6 people)

I consider it special any time I share a meal with my friends and family. There are some occasions - such as a romantic meal for two or celebrating with a few friends – when I like to make an even greater effort to add something extra to the occasion.

Depending on the time available, you may also wish to have fun by personalizing your guests' glasses - see Delicious Drinks, page 34.

To make your table more interesting, fill up hollowed out pumpkins and butternut squashes with pretty leaves and flowers; and instead of just candles, fill mini pumpkins, or oranges with tea lights - see The Charm of Candles (page 26) for ideas.

And if you are entertaining more than four people, brighten your table and make your guests feel welcome by having name tags at their place settings - see the Place Settings, page 23.

You can impress your guests with the suggested menus in this section. These light and luxurious dishes can be prepared in advance. Here are a few ideas:

&Oℭ

- Chestnut soup - see page 100
- Oven baked salmon with warm honey dill and fresh lime dressing - see page 108
- Crispy green salad
- Boiled new potatoes
- No-bake cranberry cheesecake – see page 173

&Oℭ

- Pan-seared scallops with oven-roasted tomatoes - see page 115
- Persian style chicken kebab - see page 87
- Aduki beans salsa - see page 140
- Mediterranean roasted vegetables with saffron & chestnuts - see page 146
- Served with fresh herb crème fraiche
- Pecan pie - served with ice cream - see page 179

&Oℭ

- Aromatic spinach and coconut soup - see page 97
- Sliced beef fillet with horseradish sauce - see page 91
- Oven-roasted baby potatoes - see page 77
- Char-grilled vegetables - see page 147
- Blueberry and strawberry tart with vanilla yoghurt - see page 183

- ॐ Mixed green salad with avocado
- ॐ Pan-roasted duck breast with pomegranate and walnut sauce - see page 120
- ॐ Fragrant Turmeric and cinnamon rice-see page 133
- ॐ Al dente sugar snap peas
- ॐ Platter of exquisite petits fours surrounded with juicy red berries - see page 176

Dinner Parties for Larger Gatherings

(for 6 - 12 people)

Entertaining and cooking for a fairly large group requires some extra effort but is not as challenging as you might imagine. With a bit of advance preparation, you can make it a special event which is a delight for you and your guests.

Your menu does not need to be elaborate, and you can create a pleasant and cosy atmosphere by drawing on the colours of the season and decorating your home and table accordingly - see Suggestions on page 19. You can make your occasion that bit more memorable by having an interesting theme - see Suggestions on page 11.

Whatever the occasion, I always try to plan parts of my menu ahead of time, with recipes that can be made in advance. Generally, I include one or more cold courses that can be completely prepared 1 - 2 days beforehand.

Once the big occasion finally arrives, canapés and cocktails are a wonderful, fun way to begin the evening. Usually, I tend to serve a selection of canapés as the first course, before my guests sit at the table.

When guests are seated, you can serve the main dish from a side table, if possible, and subsequently pass around the salad or vegetables for guests to help themselves.

Check Delicious Drinks on pages 34 - 48 for suggestions on drinks to serve.

And the prepared puddings simply require you to present your pièce de résistance, the work having been done ahead of time.

Bon appétit!

Here are a few menu ideas:

ॐ

- ॐ Asparagus and petits pois with toasted hazelnuts - see page 151
- ॐ Beef in a richly tomato-flavoured bean sauce with a crispy bread crumbs, Gruyere and rosemary topping - see page 124
- ॐ Crunchy coleslaw with light orange dressing - see page 162
- ॐ Dark chocolate and rum refrigerator cake - see page 173

A platter of:

- ❧ Mini tomatoes sandwiches with mozzarella and basil - see page 80
- ❧ Chorizo puffs –see page 83
- ❧ Cucumber / courgette with garlic and herb boursin - see page 81
- ❧ Roasted salmon teriyaki with sweet chilli and mint salsa - see page 108
- ❧ Saffron couscous with toasted flaked almonds - see page 136
- ❧ Mixed green salad
- ❧ Cranachan - see page 170

꧁꩜꧂

- ❧ Baba ghanoush served with a few rocket leaves and tomato slices on the side and warm roasted sesame pitta wedges - see pages 70, 75
- ❧ Persian style chicken kebab, - see page 87
- ❧ Mediterranean roasted vegetables with saffron, chestnuts - see page 146
- ❧ Served with fresh herb crème fraiche
- ❧ Platter of fresh fruit with passion fruit cream and crème de cassis - see page 170

꧁꩜꧂

- ❧ Chilled tomato, pepper and basil soup - see page 101
- ❧ Sliced beef fillet with horseradish and mini Yorkshire puddings - see page 91
- ❧ Char-grilled vegetables - see page 147
- ❧ Apple tart - see page 178

꧁꩜꧂

- ❧ Courgette and Gruyere soup - see page 98
- ❧ Lightly spiced grilled chicken with fragrant couscous - see page 118
- ❧ Warm chick peas salad with tomato and coriander / basil salsa - see page 140
- ❧ Carrot and cucumber salsa - see page 162
- ❧ Blueberry and strawberry tart with vanilla yoghurt - see page 183

꧁꩜꧂

- ❧ Oven-roasted baby tomatoes with crusty herb, parmesan and avocado - see page 149
- ❧ Oven-baked salmon with saffron and citrus dressing - see page 107
- ❧ Boiled new potatoes
- ❧ Carrot apple and fresh mint coleslaw - see page 160
- ❧ Pecan pie - see page 179

Buffets

What I love about buffets is that the foods are often more varied and enticing, yet they are more economical and simpler to prepare. Besides, a buffet is a great social enabler - it gets people mingling and chatting!

Do not be daunted by the prospect of catering for bigger numbers. The secret is preparation ahead of time. Buffet menus suggested on page 195 can be prepared in advance. This leaves time to spruce up your home and yourself so that when guests arrive all the work is done and you can enjoy the party.

TIPS:

- Buffets look a lot more impressive with 4 - 5 generous platters than too many plates of little things.
- Think through colours on plates - see Glorious Garnishes on page 55.
- It's better to serve a cold a buffet than a selection of lukewarm dishes that could breed bacteria.
- Finger buffets (foods that can be eaten without a knife and/or fork) are preferable. Just think things through, asking what guests need to eat in comfort.

Suggestions:

Menus:

Try to strike a balance between hot and cold items, light and substantial ones. Think of harmony when choosing your dishes. Start with the main dish/dishes, then select complementary salads, vegetables and desserts.

Food:

The variety of dishes you offer depends mainly on the number of guests. As a rough guide, try to serve 2 - 3 different meat dishes, 1 - 2 fish dishes and 1 - 2 vegetarian dishes along with 3 - 4 salads. And for puddings, offer a choice of 2 - 3.

How much food to prepare?

The more variety of dishes you offer, the smaller amount you need for each dish. For example, if you have in mind 2 - 3 meat dishes and 4 - 5 small salads, guests will most likely take 1 - 2 tablespoons of each. However, you will need to allow slightly more food per head. Most guests tend to try all dishes, particularly if the buffet is available throughout the occasion.

TIP:

- From experience, if there is a treat, such as smoked salmon, guests are tempted to take more, so cater for a little more.

Cooking

TIPS:

- If you are cooking for a crowd, you have more control over the taste and flavour of food when prepared in small batches. Cook for 10 people at a time, then chill or freeze. When it comes to cooking for a large number, it is not a question of just doubling or quadrupling quantities in a recipe, say, then letting it simmer or bake away. Liquids will not reduce at the same speed and cooking times may vary, leaving you with a watery casserole or a soggy pie.
- Never try to reheat food in too large quantities. It can take some time for the heat to reach the centre and the outside will become overcooked, so divide into smaller batches to heat thoroughly.

Your Table

A dining table laid with care makes any occasion less ordinary, which makes presentation so important, thus embellishing your loving labours. To make your table welcoming, see suggestions in Setting a Beautiful Table on page 21.

TIPS:

- A pretty flag can be made with cocktail sticks and a coloured Post-It note to let your guests know which country provided the idea for your choice of food
- It is very important to place the table in a way that the guests can reach food easily.
- Do not place your table in the sunny corner of the room or next to a radiator because this is a fast way to spoil your carefully prepared food.
- I usually lay the table in this order: Plates, green salads with dressings nearby, meat and fish dishes with the relevant sauces next to them, other salads, bread and butter, and finally cutlery and napkins.
- Ensure that plates are set out where guests begin to queue.
- Place the more lavish dishes such as platters of sliced beef fillet or seafood at the end of buffet line as people tend to take a more generous portion of the first couple of dishes from the start of the line.
- Never pile serving platters too high or fill dishes to the brim because food will spill. Refill dishes as necessary, especially when serving hot food.
- Cut pies and cakes into portions before placing on the table. Make things easy for your guests to enjoy helping themselves.

- Keep cold dishes refrigerated. Half an hour before your guests arrive, take the meat and salads to the table and just before serving take seafood there too.
- Keep cold food tightly covered until it is to be served. Each dish should have its own serving utensil, preferably on a small plate nearby and so that the spoon, after a few servings, does not get lost in the dish.
- Garnish only at the last minute so that everything looks fresh.

GENERAL TIPS:

- Make sure you have people to help you with food, drinks and clearing plates. At least one helper per 20 guests is ideal.
- Be ready for occasional mishaps, such as spilt wine. Mop the stain with cold water, then top with several layers of absorbent kitchen paper and leave until moisture stops leaking from the table cover or carpet.
- Decide ahead of time where to stack dirty plates. A kitchen over-flowing with washing-up looks unsightly.
- Stock up on rubbish bags and dish cloths for clearing up and cleaning after your buffet party.

More than anything, be a relaxed host and enjoy your own buffet party, knowing that everything has been thought through.

Happy entertaining!

BUFFET MENUS

A table laden with appetizing and colourful dishes allows your guests to help themselves and lets you mingle with guests in a leisurely fashion.

Here are a few suggested menus offering a blend of styles and flavours. These will give you some useful ideas on how to entertain elegantly and easily on any budget. I always serve a crispy green salad with my buffet

༄༅

- Smoked chicken and mango salad - see page 119
- Cold meat platter
- Quinoa with aduki beans salsa - see page 136
- Crunchy coleslaw with light orange dressing - see page 162.
- Waldorf salad –see page 159
- Dark chocolate & rum refrigerator cake - see page 173
- Pecan pie –see page 179

༄༅

- Parmesan & sage meatballs with chorizo sauce (allow 3 - 5 meatballs per head) - see page 129
- Seafood platter
- Boiled new potatoes
- Persian style couscous with pomegranate seeds & fresh mint - see page 135
- Cannellini, beetroot & apple salad - see page 143
- Selection of cheese and biscuits
- Platter of fresh fruit with passion fruit cream with elderflower cordial - see page 170

༄༅

- Lightly spiced grilled chicken (allow 2 - 3 pieces of chicken per head) - see page 88
- Baby potatoes with fresh chopped dill and buttermilk dressing - see page 158
- Platter of finely sliced tomatoes drizzled with olive oil and squeeze of lime juice, garnished with roughly torn basil
- Finely sliced roast beef fillet with horseradish sauce (400 g of roast beef fillet makes about 16 - 18 slices, allowing approximately 2 - 3 slices per head). See page 91.
- Aduki beans salsa - see page 140
- Cranachan - see page 170
- Apple tart - see page 178

- French beans and petits pois with a tarragon dressing - see page 151
- Sea food platter
- Platter of finely sliced roast chilli duck breasts (250 g of duck breast makes about 8 slices, allowing about 2 - 3 slices per head) - see page 89
- Aduki beans salsa - see page 140
- Chocolate, almond and pear tart made without eggs - see page 184
- Blueberry and strawberry tart with vanilla yoghurt - see page 183

Final Thoughts

The warm glow you feel after hosting a good party can fill you with energy for days - the kind of energy which helps you to achieve a whole lot of other things!

The world seems a happier place when you feel the warmth and support of friends and you feel better inside too. Never forget that a pleasant evening shared with companions can more than double your joy and halve your sorrows.

Sharing a meal is a timeless ritual in extending the hand of friendship. The love and care you put into making that delicious meal can be fun and therapeutic. Even preparing a simple earthy soup can lift you out of your everyday concerns. As you concentrate on peeling, chopping and seasoning, the cares of the day gently fade away. The simplest dish can become a pleasure to others and a source of pride for you, knowing how good it feels to watch others enjoying something you have created.

Recipes in this book are kept simple in order to savour good natural ingredients. They do not demand any great kitchen skills. Even if you're just starting out in entertaining, you can quickly become a great host on a very modest budget.

The suggestions and tips given on planning, ambience (especially the colours), garnishes, food and drinks will encourage you to be more and more creative.

I hope this book will help you discover the spirit and joy of home entertaining.

All you need is love, care and patience, and every occasion will be a pleasure.

Conversion Tables

If you prefer to use US measurements the following conversion lists will help you.
All these are approximate conversions, which have either been rounded up or down.

A Guide for American Users:

Metric	Imperial	American
450 g	1 lb butter or fat	2 cups
450 g	1 lb flour	4 cups
450 g	1 lb granulated or caster sugar	2 cups
300 g	12 oz golden syrup	1 cup
350 g	14 oz rice	2 cups
450 g	1 lb dried fruit	3 cups
450 g	1 lb chopped or minced meat	2 cups
450 g	1 lb lentils	2 cups
50 g	2 oz soft bread crumbs	1 cup
10 g	½ oz flour	2 tablespoons
25 g	1 oz flour	¼ cup
25 g	1 oz sugar	2 tablespoons
10 g	½ oz butter	1 tablespoon
25 g	1 oz golden syrup	1 tablespoon
100 g	4 oz grated cheese	1 cup
100 g	4 oz chopped nuts	1 cup

Liquid Measures

150 ml	¼ pint water, milk, etc.	2/3 cup
275 ml	½ pint water	1¼ cups
570 ml	1 pint water	2½ cups

Note:

A British pint is 20 fluid ounces, while an American pint is 16 fluid ounces

Measurements

5 mm	¼ inch
1 cm	½ inch
2.5 cm	1 inch

Index

Acknowledgements

My heartfelt thanks to those who advised, helped and encouraged me.

My editor Kate McNeilly, my food photographer Kevin Wooding, Lizzie May, Vibeke Dahl and Olivier Bourseau for his tips on wine and champagne, and friends too numerous to mention for being food testers when I was writing this book.

Finally, my special thanks to Joyce McKibbin, Denise Bruce and my family - Richard, my husband, my son Justin Driskill as adviser and to my son Gerry, daughters in-law Elle and Kathy and my sisters Farangis and Soraya and their husbands.

Mahin's Story

Mahin Driskill became passionate about food and a huge fan of home entertaining entirely by accident. Growing up in Persia, her dream was to work for the United Nations, to travel the world and to make it a better place. With a sense of adventure and seeking further education, she persuaded her very conservative parents to let her pursue her studies in London in the mid-seventies.

Once there, she soon fell in love and married a Texan, entered a different world and totally unknown territory - a place she had never been before and had no desire to be - the kitchen!
It became her responsibility to host and cater for her husband's many business associates. She could not cook and was not particularly interested in food. An array of cookbooks and persistence were her only allies. Her early culinary efforts were far from successful … but her desire to be a good cook and hostess grew strong.

Meanwhile, married life - and her husband's job - took her from London to Scotland, America, Norway, Scotland and back to London. As they moved from place to place, from home to home with two young sons, entertaining became her lifeline, her way of getting to know new people wherever she lived. Mahin's parties, however, were still like a dry roast. They fell short on the gravy of entertainment. Her determination to succeed grew ever stronger. She enrolled in local cookery courses every time she arrived in a new country. As her cooking improved, so did her morale and she became interested in personal development. She took courses in nutrition, Feng Shui and many other things and took on board the wisdom of these diverse disciplines. Over time, she started weaving this knowledge into her parties.

Travelling gave Mahin new ideas and inspiration. She began experimenting and merged dishes from the West with the gentle, fragrant herbs and spices of the Middle East of her birth place and created new exciting recipes. Initially, she used her degree in Marketing and Management to pursue a career in finance. However, the creative side of her personality longed to be expressed. It was this that provided her with the impetus to start her own catering company in 1986. Mahin's reputation as a stylish caterer spread far and wide and clients highly praised her "elegant, simple and exclusive flair."

If learning how to cook and entertain had served her well throughout her marriage, it became her mainstay when she went through a bitter divorce. In spite of everything, her food remained sweet and delicious and she continued to thrive as a businesswoman.

Mahin believes that honing her home entertaining skills was better than any personal development course. It enhanced her creative side, boosted her confidence and gave her the skills to survive on her own and make great friends. Her thirst for self-improvement led her to join Toastmasters International where her leadership skills improved so much that, over time, she became President of London Athenians and met many people from diverse backgrounds with more opportunities to entertain and be entertained. Meanwhile, she married a wonderful man who appreciates good food as much as she does. When asked what she does, Mahin says: *"I take away the fear of home entertaining and inspire individuals to make their home a more inviting place and provide delicious food. That way, they can proudly open the door of their home and use home entertainment as a time-honoured way to build, cement and enrich relationships."*

Even though she is enthralled by the alchemy of cooking, Mahin believes that home entertainment is also about artistic pursuits and the little touches that make such a difference in creating an ambience for the whole experience of sharing a meal which gives and provides enjoyment.

A strong desire to share her love of cooking and entertaining resulted in this book being written. It captures only part of a lifetime's experience of tried and tested recipes and tips and all the things that go into making home entertainment wonderful, giving it that wow-factor that makes each occasion a joy.